Almost Home

Helping Kids Move from Homelessness to Hope

KEVIN RYAN AND
TINA KELLEY

WILEY
John Wiley & Sons, Inc.

*Dedicated to the young people who struggle on the
streets, and the loving adults who lift them up*

The book is printed on acid-free paper. ∞

Copyright © 2012 by Covenant House. All rights reserved
Interior photos: © Timothy Ivy

The lines from "The Opening of Eyes," from *Songs for Coming Home*, by David Whyte, are printed
with permission from Many Rivers Press, http://www.davidwhyte.com, © Many Rivers Press,
Langley, Washington.

Cover image: © Jan Sonnenmair

Published by John Wiley & Sons, Inc., Hoboken, New Jersey
Published simultaneously in Canada

For general information about our other products and services, please contact our Customer Care
Department within the United States at (800) 762-2974, outside the United States at (317) 572-
3993 or fax (317) 572-4002.

Wiley also publishes its books in a variety of electronic formats and by print-on-demand. Some
content that appears in standard print versions of this book may not be available in other formats.
For more information about Wiley products, visit us at www.wiley.com.

Library of Congress Cataloging-in-Publication Data:

Ryan, Kevin.
    Almost home : helping kids move from homelessness to hope / Kevin Ryan and Tina Kelley.
        p. cm.
    Includes index.
    ISBN 978-1-118-23047-3 (pbk); ISBN 978-1-118-28698-2 (ebk);
    ISBN 978-1-118-28295-3 (ebk); ISBN 978-1-118-28403-2 (ebk)
        1. Homeless children—United States.   2. Homeless youth—United States.
        3. Homeless children—Canada.   4. Homeless youth—Canada. I. Kelley, Tina. II. Title.
    HV4505.R798   2012
    362.77'56920820973—dc23

                                                                                    2012017212

Printed in the United States of America

10   9   8   7   6   5   4   3   2   1

Contents

Photo gallery begins on page 143.

Acknowledgments

We could never have written this book without the openness and generosity of the six young people who told us their life stories. They spent hundreds of hours walking and talking with us for much of the past three years, and we are deeply grateful. Their stories would have been far different without the devotion and dedication of the men and women who cared *for* them and *about* them, day in and day out, including the counselors and other staff members of Covenant House who also shared their time and insights with us.

We heard in the voices of so many kids a burgeoning hope that is the legacy of Sister Mary Rose McGeady, D.C., and Jim Harnett, who spent most of their lives fighting for homeless and forgotten young people. They kept company with those who lit the way forward as stewards of this movement to end the exploitation and suffering of young people, including Dorothy McGuinness, Joan Lambert, Bob Cardany, Bruce Henry, Sister Tricia Cruise, Pat Connors, Priscilla and Dick Marconi, Bill and Peggy Montgoris, L. Edward and Irene Shaw, Ralph and Jane Pfeiffer, Dick and Priscilla Schmeelk, Brian D. McAuley, and Denis P. Coleman.

We hold great esteem for men and women across Canada and the United States who devote part of their lives to loving other people's children and giving them alternatives to street life. This is especially true for the Covenant House staff, who do difficult and incredible work, every day of the year.

Our agent, Andrew Blauner, one of our first and most important yay-sayers, buoyed us when we needed it, and Tom Miller, our editor at Wiley, believed in this project in a way that touched us deeply. We are beyond grateful to them. C. Allen Parker, Esq., Paul Saunders, Esq., Stuart Gold, Esq., and their colleagues at Cravath, Swaine & Moore, and the constant, patient, and wise John Ducoff, Esq., provided us expert legal advice and were advocates of the first order for our work. Liz Lewis, Jayne Bigelsen, Mary Ann Simulinas, Elisabeth Lean, Molly Ladd, and the Covenant House Institute provided research assistance; Patrice Ingra juggled schedules with inimitable good humor; and it's safe to say we were each blessed with a coauthor of great good cheer and endurance.

We are deeply indebted to the experts who shared their original research and wisdom with us, from across two countries, including those who are mentioned in these pages and so many others—experts in the kids we write about; experts in the care of the mind, the heart, and the spirit; and experts in wise policies for the benefit of young people. Thanks for your insights and for helping us reach the conclusions we did.

Across Canada and the United States, Covenant House executive directors opened our eyes to the suffering of homeless young people in their states and provinces, and we are thankful to each of them: Allison Ashe in Georgia, Dan Brannen in the District of Columbia, Ruth daCosta and Bruce Rivers in Toronto, Deirdre Cronin in Alaska, Jim Gress in Florida, Cordella Hill in Pennsylvania, Sam Joseph in Michigan, Jim Kelly in Louisiana, Jerry Kilbane and Jim White in New York, George Lozano in California, Ronda G. Robinson in Texas, Jill Rottmann in New Jersey, Krista Thompson in Vancouver, and Sue Wagener in Missouri.

We developed an abiding esteem for the great human rights activists who inspired us in their fight against child trafficking, including Menin Capellin, Carolina Escobar Sarti, Maria Jose

Arguello, Sofia Almazan, Hugh Organ Sr., Nancy Brown, Norma Ramos, Andrea Powell, and Rachel Lloyd.

Thanks to Tyler Perry, Jon Bon Jovi, Natalie Grant, and Laura Bush, who helped us over the last three years to reach so many more kids, and to Cory Booker for his passion and vision.

We are grateful to our friend Jim Burke, who generously gave us a peaceful place to write and meet in the summer of 2011, and to the talented and good-humored Timothy Ivy, whose photographs reveal the heart and power of the special young people of Covenant House in New York.

We are thankful to the board of Covenant House International: Phil Andryc, Barbara P. Bush, Andrew P. Bustillo, John F. Byren, Brian M. Cashman, Paul A. Danforth, Mark J. Hennessy, Capathia Y. Jenkins, Tracy S. Jones-Walker, Drew A. Katz, Janet M. Keating, Thomas M. McGee, Brian T. "BT" McNicholl, Anne M. Milgram, Karla Mosley, Liz Murray, John C. Pescatore, Brother Raymond Sobocinski, Thomas D. Woods, and Strauss Zelnick. And to the board members of Covenant Houses across Canada and the United States, thank you for your dedication to creating opportunities for children and youth.

To the millions of special people who have contributed to the Covenant House movement, believing that every young person deserves the opportunity to shine, regardless of the circumstances of their birth, thank you. Huge thanks to our Broadway friends for inspiring us with their time, talent, and dedication to homeless young people, especially the multitalented Neil Berg and Rita Harvey, John Asselta, Dan Walker, Carter Calvert and Roger Cohen, Lawrence Clayton, Natalie Toro, Rob Evan, Danny Zolli, Ron Bohmer and Sandra Joseph, Craig Schulman, Al Greene, and our beloved Capathia.

We thank our friends and family who provided invaluable feedback, guidance, and moral support: Liz Alanis, Molly Armstrong, Neela Banerjee, Lynn and Tom Benediktsson, Elaine Bennett, Abraham Bergman, Alison Brosnan, Lou Carlozo, Lisa Chang, Eileen Crummy, Meredith Fabian, Dan Froomkin, Scott

Hamilton, Peggy Healy (*abrazos*), Tom Kennedy, Taisha Kullman, Carlette Mack, Frith Maier, Rylee Maloles, Tom Manning, Dan McCarthy, Peggy McHale, Diane Milan, Robin Nagle, Barbara, Jerry, and Livia Newman, John O'Brien, Karl Pettijohn, Jeanne Pinder, Susan Plum (our tireless friend and reader), Ruben Porras, Tom Potenza, Susan Rabiner, Lee Roberts, Vera Roche, Tim Ryan, Emily Schifrin, Lauren Simonds, Lisa Taylor, Joan Smyth, Ruth Warner, Laura Weinberg, Richard Wexler—and Jill, Joan, and John again, for their many readings and generous input. We know both Ann Hoelle and Frank Kelley were there in spirit throughout.

To people who extended their hospitality during our travels, deep gratitude: Deirdre and Rob Cronin, Alison Kear, Mike Mills, Kevin Kerr, Roberta Degenhardt, Owen Ryan and Trevor McLaren, Al Gough and Beth Corets, Bill and Peggy Roe, Fred Weil and Kayo, Rio and Kento, Diane and Reilly Gillette, and Neela, and Karl again.

To the Ryans: Clare, Dan, Liam, John, Nora, Maggie, and Maeve; home will always be wherever you are. Thanks for happily making the Covenant House movement so much a part of our life. A special smile for Maeve for keeping it real when relaying exactly what the breeze says to the trees on a winding river in Westport. To Jim and Eileen Ryan, whose big shoulders and bigger hearts carried their sons, and to my brothers, much love, always. And a special thanks to Ellie Boddie and Joe and Kathleen Neitzey for countless sacrifices in the name of family. Most of all, to Clare, who strummed her guitar to the music of Paul McCartney, James Taylor, and the Indigo Girls during many late-night (re)writing sessions; you've multiplied life by the power of two.

To Kate and Drew Newman, who were patient when deadlines always landed smack at the end of vacations: a ton of IOUs and much gratitude. To Tish Kelley, who always encouraged the pursuit of dreams: love, thanks, and a good long laugh about it all. To Pete, who heard and read these stories many times over, asked all the right questions, and believed in just the right ways: an honorary byline and many hugs.

Foreword

—*Cory Booker,*
Mayor of Newark,
New Jersey

I've learned that real heroes usually aren't the kind of people you read about in newspapers or see on TV. Real heroes are usually the ones concerned with the least glamorous of things. In fact, I've come to believe strongly that the most heroic or biggest thing we can do in any day is a small act of kindness, decency, or love. What frustrates me is that so often we allow our inability to do the big things to undermine our determination to do the small things, those acts of kindness, decency, and love that in their aggregate over days, weeks, and years make powerful change.

My parents raised me to know this. They raised me to understand that I was the result of a vast and profound conspiracy of love. My father, for example, was born poor. In fact, he jokes now that he wasn't born poor, he was born "po"—he couldn't afford the other two letters. He was born to a single mother who couldn't take care of him, and after his grandmother couldn't take care of him either, it was the kindness and love of strangers that stabilized his life and gave him a foundation to eventually head off to college. This past Thanksgiving as my family was going around the table saying what we were thankful for, my father got a little emotional talking about his childhood and how people whose names he couldn't even remember helped him. He talked about how when he was college-age, people reached out and gave him dollar bills to ensure he could afford his first semester's tuition.

Time and time again, my parents reminded me that there were thousands of people over numerous generations who did for my family and our ancestors. All that I have now is the result not only of famous people from history, but mostly of ordinary Americans who showed extraordinary kindness—small acts that were not required of them but that they just *did*. I am proud of that part of our American history. I am proud that although I don't know their names, there were so many people who just did: they mentored and marched, they served and sacrificed, they loved.

We in this nation drink deeply from wells of freedom and liberty that we did not dig; we eat from lavish banquet tables that were prepared for us by our common ancestors. And we can either sit back and consume all that has been placed before us, or we can choose to remember. We may not remember names or dates, but we can remember this spirit, that soulfulness, the conspiracy of love that so shaped our nation and experiences. And more than remember, we can metabolize our blessings and keep the conspiracy alive.

In Newark, I often get to witness people who are the modern-day manifestation of this spirit of humility and service. I encounter and work with people who are focused on the least glamorous of things and yet make some of the most profound differences in our city. In fact, I am proud that the spirit that took my father, from a "po" boy without a home, to a college graduate, IBM executive, and even father of two children is alive and well.

Three blocks away from City Hall is a place called Covenant House. The people there work with youth, and I believe they see in each one the same potential, promise, dignity, and hope that people saw when they looked at my dad back in the 1940s and 1950s. They serve homeless youth, but I actually think that through what they do, they serve us all.

They do the wonderfully unglamorous things; they perform significant and unyielding small acts of kindness, decency, and love. They empower lives and change destinies. They know that it actually doesn't take all that much to keep a young life from veering far off track.

In the stories you'll find in this book, there are several crossroads, where a kid's fate turns on the next encounter: will a kind person come along, or will it be a mugger, or a hater, or worse? Sometimes it's an elderly couple who give a kid a lift to a homeless shelter. Sometimes it's a counselor who says, "You look like you need to talk." Sometimes it's a barber who sees potential and hires someone fresh out of jail, lending him tools of the trade; or it's a friend's mom who lets a kid crash in the guest room for a couple weeks. Sometimes it's a coach or a teacher or a volunteer who provides the belief and encouragement that lights a fire in a young heart. None of these actions cost the grownups all that much, but each act of kindness and love from a humble hero can form a turning point for a kid who needs direction.

At Covenant House, the stakes are higher than at many other places. Covenant House workers have one main goal: to love kids the world too often calls unlovable; they want to keep the conspiracy of love alive for everyone, to ensure that no one is left without. It's not always easy work, but they try hard to bring open and loving hearts to kids who, often, don't believe that adults can possibly care. No one has before, so why should some stranger start now?

I've encountered other disadvantaged young people in my travels; I've seen their uncertainty, or worse, the way their eyes seem to shut down in the face of poverty and hopelessness. But at Covenant House, I see enthusiasm in the eyes of the young people, their hope, and how they know big things are possible for them.

It's the ones who arrive at the shelter who are, in some ways, lucky and the ones most likely to succeed, the ones most likely to

contribute to the well-being and strength of all of us. By definition, they care enough about their future and their safety to come
in from the dangers of their homes or the street. Their instinct for
self-preservation hasn't been pummeled out of them yet. Some
have heard about the shelter through a friend or a family member,
which means they may have a social network in place.

It's the isolated, defeated kids, the kids in cities and towns
without youth shelters, who make me worry—they don't have anywhere to make a home or find a community of support. They're the
ones who are most vulnerable to the dangers of the streets.

I've seen too many of our kids, young and uncertain, wondering if they will ever have a fair shot at attaining their dreams. They
wonder if the world is a place that will welcome them or smack
them down—again.

Fortunately there are many ways grownups can help, many
ways our small acts can make big differences. We can advocate for
homeless kids, wherever they are, and we can simply become more
aware by reading up on ways to prevent youth homelessness, such
as those described in this book.

I am lucky. I had a father and mother who provided me a
home; I had a father who had a community that would not let him
fail when he was young. And we all encountered a world where
we were taught that we had worth, not one that made us feel
worthless.

Too many Covenant House kids grow up without any of those
blessings. They get mad at the world, and at the people who have
hurt them. They have what Kevin Ryan calls "dynamite in their
stomachs," an emotional storm that can be calmed by love or hope,
but only if they find it.

I have a stubborn faith in us as a community and nation. I
believe that we can give every kid these basics: a feeling of worth,
a home, and a pathway to advance their dreams. We can break the
cycle of despair and hopelessness kids can get caught in. In fact it

is not a question of can we—it is a question of will we. I believe, collectively, that we will break the cycle of poverty and homelessness. Covenant House has a mighty recipe for doing that: unconditional respect and love, help with schooling and finding jobs and apartments, assistance with mental and physical health needs, and a shared belief in our children's future and their ability to follow their dreams.

We can't lose a generation to homelessness. With the loss of those children, we would lose all they could contribute to strengthening our communities. That doesn't have to happen. It can't happen, not on our watch. Generations to come depend on our success.

I know that those folks who helped my dad may not have imagined my brother, me, and our generation, but their conspiracy of love back then helped us to serve, give, and love now. Let's keep the conspiracy going and make real on the promise of our nation that our children speak of every single day in a chorus of conviction, when they say those last six words of the pledge: With Liberty and Justice for All.

Preface
Years to Understand the Light

—*Kevin Ryan*

I came to New York City in the fall of 1992 as a newly minted lawyer fresh from Georgetown Law Center, hoping to save the world and help homeless and runaway youth. My charge was to provide legal aid to homeless young people in family court, housing court, or any of the civil venues that overflowed with poor people.

I arrived at Covenant House, which this year celebrates its fortieth anniversary, just as the dust was settling from the worst scandal to hit an American charity in many years. Truth is, there wasn't a long line of applicants eager to work at Covenant House back then. In 1989, Covenant House's founder, Father Bruce Ritter, had been accused of having sexual relationships with several young people at the shelter, of keeping a secret trust fund, and of further financial improprieties. He was never charged with a crime, but he stepped down as head of the agency in February 1990. That was shortly before the Manhattan district attorney said he would not bring criminal charges against Father Ritter. A report commissioned by Covenant House's Board of Directors described "cumulative evidence . . . supporting the allegations of sexual misconduct" and added, "Father Ritter exercised unacceptably poor judgment in his relations with certain residents." The report, supervised by a former

New York City police commissioner, concluded, "[I]f Father Ritter had not resigned, the termination of the relationship between him and Covenant House would have been required."

With Covenant House's future hanging in the balance, the Board of Directors hired a new president, a forceful social worker and Roman Catholic nun, to save the day, and that she did. Sister Mary Rose McGeady arrived in 1990, clear-eyed about the task before her: thousands of staff members, volunteers, and donors felt betrayed, curtailing their support of Covenant House just as the economic recession of the early 1990s caused a surge in teen homelessness. She implemented rigorous new standards of transparency and accountability that the state attorney general had insisted on, and she spent the first several years restoring confidence in the charity. Thanks to her work, after a free fall in donations in 1990, charitable contributions to the agency grew again, allowing her to more than double the number of Covenant Houses in the United States, Canada, and Latin America.

Unlike most of Covenant House's supporters at that time, I had not learned about homeless teenagers from Father Ritter or Sister Mary Rose. My tutor was a young woman named Clare, whom I knew from my undergraduate days at Catholic University and who had decided to become a full-time volunteer at Covenant House in New Orleans after graduation. I was so touched by the ways the isolated young people of the French Quarter inhabited her heart, I signed up for a tour of duty myself and soon resolved to make it part of my life's mission or, more accurately, our life's mission. By the time I finished law school, Clare and I were married and had an infant son.

Covenant House in New York City was a revelation to me. I had never dined with teenagers grappling with despair, until that Thanksgiving when I met three boys who had just learned at our health center that they had tested positive for HIV and were singing bits of pop songs they wanted played at their funerals. I had no idea that some fifteen- and sixteen-year-olds endured serial rapes for the benefit of corner pimps, until I met them in the shelter that first Christmas, two of them pregnant. I just didn't realize so many young people were homeless and alone. I did not understand that children—in real life, as opposed to in the movies—were ever stolen from their families, forced into servitude, and driven to life on the streets. That is, until I met Binnie. She was the first teenager who asked for my help at Covenant House, back in 1992. Picked up by the Port Authority Police, she was brought to Covenant House in a puddle of tears. Reeking of dirt and urine, she was shy, anxious, full of fear, and unable to hold her head up.

Lost in her misery, Binnie was a slight figure, eyes bloodshot from crying, and for good reason. As a young teenager, she had been taken from her home by extended family members when her mother fell ill. They withdrew her from school, forced her to do all of the family's cooking and cleaning, and forbade her to leave the house. By the time she was sixteen, her family had offered her up to the son of a powerful neighbor, who repeatedly raped her. She escaped one night, made her way to John F. Kennedy International Airport in New York City, and scavenged for food in the trash cans, sleeping for more than a week among the terminals until the police found her and brought her to Covenant House.

Binnie's life allowed me to confront human suffering in a new way. Yet even as the white-hot spotlight of her reality illuminated dark corners for me, I still could not see the fullness of her life. I did not know it at the time, but much like the Alaskan halibut caught by Paulie Robbins, whose story inspired me and broke my heart during the reporting for this book, I was developing a blind spot at Covenant House. The halibut has two eyes on one cheek, and it is unable to see half the world. I was just like that, blind to the other side of the bridge where the kids were heading. I came to know mostly the darkness and the shadows, and it would be years before I began to understand the light.

Then one day I ran into Binnie at a diner in midtown Manhattan. She was almost unrecognizable, though she had not gained more than five pounds or grown an inch since I met her. I remembered her as a hunched teenager, but now she was a tall young woman in her early twenties, poised and smiling, head held high. She wore a bright-blue waitress dress with a white apron, and her face glowed. She told me about her determination to become a registered nurse and work in a hospital. The diner salary helped pay her way through nursing school, so she did not need to rely on loans. She was dating a boy she had met at church, and he was kind and loving. She said she was happy in this new life. I told her she was amazing.

Whether or not she knew it at the time, Binnie planted a seed that sparked a handful of new questions for me as I walked back to the shelter.

How could a young person, abandoned by everyone around her and left to sleep in an airport, go on to dedicate her life to others as a nurse? How do young people transcend the sort of violence and rejection that overshadowed Binnie's childhood? How do kids prosper after suffering alone on the streets for months, sometimes years? How could travelers pass by that heap of a girl sleeping at JFK airport without noticing her? And when they do notice young people like her, how can they help?

The best answers, of course, lay in the lives of the young people themselves and in the acts of compassion by complete strangers that inspire transformation. I cowrote this book to find these answers, tell these stories, and, I hope, encourage people of goodwill to believe they can make a difference in the lives of young homeless people, helping them on their way to a brighter future.

In the darkness, inspiration is not merely a flashlight; it is the oxygen that keeps us breathing. I have seen it time and again, starting with the many years I worked with homeless, runaway, and trafficked youth at Covenant House. But this is not limited to Covenant House. I spent seven years working to reform child protection systems and helping to launch a global support program with the United Nations to reduce malaria deaths, which at the time claimed more than 1 million lives a year, mostly African children. When I returned to head Covenant House in 2009, I did so savoring the optimism and determination of the men and the women who had blazed trails during these years, achieving significant improvements in New Jersey's child welfare system and stunning reductions in malaria mortality in Africa. My colleagues sent me back to Covenant House with a gift: the belief that anything is possible if people are inspired to make it so.

Less than a year ago, I received a note from Binnie, now a mother to three young children and a nurse in the pediatric intensive care unit at a top hospital. "My dear Kevin," she wrote, "I hope you had a very good Thanksgiving with all the children. We had a very nice day here. I have so many things to be grateful for, something I never forget when I see all the sick little ones here at the hospital." Times were tight, she said, because her husband was looking for work, but she and her family had all that they needed, and she was sending fifty dollars to buy a warm meal for children at Covenant House.

"I hope it helps," she signed off. It did, in more ways than one. I hope her story and the stories of young people like her remind us that we can change the world, one bold kindness at a time.

Preface
Help and the Homing Instinct

—Tina Kelley

When Kevin spoke about his desire to coauthor a book about homeless kids, it sounded like a dream job. The challenges inherent in this project remind me a bit of those I found in writing 121 "Portraits of Grief" at the *New York Times*, short descriptions of the people silenced forever on September 11, 2001. How do you present a multifaceted life in a way that honors it most authentically? How can you write about searing loss—of life, of innocence, of childhood—while still inviting people in to read more, to look through the pain and find common ground? Our mission was to introduce some exceptional young people so that readers could feel at home with them, understand their stories, and know them by name, not as "those kids," a phrase that seldom leads anywhere good.

I had volunteered at the Covenant House shelter in New York City in the late 1980s and admired the courage of its residents then. Now, as the young people in this book welcomed me into their stories, they convinced me of the commonalities among us all. We all wanted to go to the prom, we all love our music, we all have shaken our heads at grownups, and we all have had people who believe in us.

Yet the mettle of these six young adults—Paulie, Muriel, Benjamin, Creionna, Keith, and Meagan—has been tempered by the sickness in their homes and the greed of their exploiters. I wondered how on earth I would have made it through the adversity they faced as babies or toddlers or young children, through no moral failing of their own. Those circumstances, which might well have flattened me, often left them vilified and victimized, but here they were, speaking frankly, often smiling. I felt as if I were interviewing marathon runners, while I had never even jogged around the block.

During my decade at the *Times*, I wrote many stories about controversies involving marginalized or voiceless individuals, stories on polarized communities and courageous struggles against popular opinion. I reported on the health problems of a Native American tribe living near a Superfund site; a transgender vocational school principal in a rural town; and the lives of children waiting to be adopted out of foster care. I also covered Kevin's efforts to reform New Jersey's troubled child welfare system, when he was the statewide child advocate and then the commissioner of the Department of Children and Families. All of these articles, I see now, involved people whose sense of home had been severely shaken.

I never knew how much home mattered to kids who had dangerous family lives. I used to think children would be glad to land in a safe and friendly foster home, where they could expect an end to the beatings and careless insults. From working on this book, though, I see that the pull of home, even a scary and sadistic one, is deeply ingrained in us all.

Slowly, I came to understand why Benjamin, when he was four, would try to cross a four-lane road to return to the mother who had burned him—to him, she was also the source of the first comfort he had ever known, and he hoped beyond hope that she would comfort him again. I was amazed by the forgiveness and generosity Meagan showed to her family, who had kicked her to the curb. And

Keith startled me when he turned the other cheek to his mother, who, he was told, had killed his father and then abandoned her three tiny sons. I remembered the philosopher Blaise Pascal, who wrote, "The heart has reasons that reason knows nothing of."

It is hard to spend time with young people in Covenant House without fuming about and grieving for their parents. Certainly, we hear more of the kid's side of the story, not the details of a mother's frustrations over a broken curfew or a father's anger about skipped school. But to hear a child talk about a parent's cruelty stretches the limits of compassion.

It helps to remember that the parents, too, are God's children, God's broken children, perhaps, but full of their own dreams, regrets, talents, missteps, and humanity as well. What went wrong to make them hear voices in their heads? What demons were they fleeing, what memories were they reenacting when they hit and hurt their children so deeply?

Many Covenant House kids carry snapshots of themselves as little ones, and these can be more painful to see than any report in a case file. Here is a chubby, pony-tailed Creionna—isn't there a way to wave a wand and give this toddler the future she deserves? Here's a picture of Paulie, catching halibut in Alaska, before most of the beatings, before his family imploded, before he quit school. His eyes show all of the promise of a kid who is smart enough to earn an equivalency diploma after attending only a few months of high school. If only someone had stepped in when these kids were young, to give them the right kind of love and attention to help them flourish! But that didn't happen.

Jim White, who runs one of our largest Covenant Houses, in New York City, says in this book, "Sometimes we run and we run, and only home can make us whole. We have to turn back and make peace in order to move forward." A true home, serving as both springboard and anchor, has been stolen from the kids in this book, but somehow they have transcended that deficit.

They survive. They start to thrive, building their own new lives and new relationships, with so little preparation and modeling from their earlier years. With the generous gift of their time and explanations, these three young men and three young women at the heart of our book, and the adults who have guided them, have helped me see that they are, in a word, crucial. So are their stories.

As I researched more about homeless young people, I saw how they try to fly under the radar, keeping themselves invisible. Many of us don't notice homeless young people at all. We walk past street musicians or kids asking for spare change, not thinking twice when we see a teenager leaning against a bus station wall. Kids like them sit next to us on the subway or fold our clothes at the Gap, yet their secret strengths, their humor and hopefulness, remain hidden.

They don't want us to know they have nowhere to go. The advocacy community has found it nearly impossible to obtain an accurate count of homeless young people, in part because they find it safer and less embarrassing to hide. Homeless kids tend to stay with friends, disappear into the woods or the alleys, and generally avoid attention, to steer clear of the people who might use, rob, or harm them. Some don't want to be sent to foster care. Some are ashamed of their unwashed bodies and ill-fitting clothes, while they live off scraps and try to make it to school or work. Those who are being prostituted are kept hidden by their exploiters and made to lie about their age if stopped by the police. That's all the more reason their journeys must be understood.

What is lost as these young people have gone unnoticed? It's hard to help someone if you don't know he or she exists. It's hard for these kids to exist, literally, if more people don't help. And with a little help and hope received in times of crisis, they can have the independent and healthy lives they deserve. My wish is that the young people in this book and the many more whom Covenant House serves can find a home in your heart and, with the help of others like you, a loving home of their own, at last.

Introduction

Homeless young people largely remain invisible, except to the strangers who step forward to offer a hand and, in doing so, change their world. This book describes the courage of six tenacious young people across North America, but it is just as much about the adults who gave them a chance—sometimes working within Covenant House, sometimes not. They look rather average: a New Orleans cook who has spent her life feeding other women's children; a New Jersey executive searching for a deeper meaning to life; an Alaskan single mother battling to keep hope alive after her husband leaves; a Vancouver nun at war with traffickers and pimps; a Texas football family, scooping up a new son from the ruins of a violent childhood; and the social workers, foster parents, and friends around the United States and Canada who care for children who have nowhere to go. They may not have trophies on their mantels for it, but they have each helped guide a young person into the great promise of his or her life.

For the last forty years, there's been no shortage of stories to be found at Covenant House, the largest charity of its kind in the Americas helping homeless, runaway, and trafficked children and youth. Each night about thirteen hundred kids stay at the charity's shelters in the United States and Canada, and each young person could weave a compelling narrative, though few such stories are ever heard by a large audience. Covenant House shelters help kids in Anchorage, Atlanta, Atlantic City, Detroit, Fort Lauderdale, Houston, Los Angeles, New Orleans, New York City, Newark, Oakland, Orlando, Philadelphia, St. Louis, Toronto, Vancouver, and Washington, D.C. Each year Covenant House shelters more than eleven thousand youth, most between sixteen and twenty-one, and it reaches more than fifty-six thousand, including those who are helped by its crisis hotline and outreach vans that search the streets and alleys of dangerous neighborhoods, looking for kids in need. In New Jersey, Covenant House provides shelter for young mothers in Elizabeth and for young people with mental health issues in Montclair, with plans for a storefront opening in Camden and outreach efforts under way in Jersey City and Asbury Park.

Beyond the United States and Canada, each night Covenant House also takes care of an additional four hundred younger children, including many trafficking survivors, in safe houses and shelters in Managua, Nicaragua; Tegucigalpa, Honduras; Guatemala City, Guatemala; and Mexico City, Mexico. Covenant House is known in these countries as Casa Alianza, and this extraordinary human rights work across Latin America merits a book of its own; stay tuned. This book focuses on the experiences of homeless children and youth in the United States and Canada.

Each year as many as two million young people in the United States face an episode of homelessness; in Canada, an estimated sixty-five thousand young people are homeless. While milk cartons have shown the faces of missing kids whose parents are panicked and heartsick over their absence, who looks for the adolescents who get kicked out of their homes and land in the streets? More than half of the unaccompanied young people interviewed by the Family and Youth Services Bureau of the United States Administration for Children and Families said their parents either told them to leave home or knew they were leaving and didn't care. These kids are lonesome and low on resources, needing a room to sleep in, food for breakfast, and a sympathetic ear.

Almost 40 percent of homeless people in the United States are under eighteen. Many live with at least one parent, but some young people become homeless when they believe the streets offer a safer alternative to abusive, drug-dependent, or mentally ill families. Some never had a consistent home, because they were tossed through the foster care system, never adopted, then left alone at age eighteen. Some are kicked out of their homes right after telling their parents they are gay or pregnant, and some are considered old enough to make it on their own when an extra mouth to feed is too expensive or when their mental health issues cause too much trouble. In any case, the myth of the star-struck adolescent who runs away to Hollywood or Times Square to find a glamorous new life is largely out of date. Young people too often run away from something awful, not toward something hopeful.

Recently, during the worst U.S. recession since the Great Depression, their chances of finding work and an affordable apartment are slim at best. According to a February report from the Pew Research Center, the percentage of employed young adults ages eighteen to twenty-four fell from 62.4 in 2007 to 54.3 in 2011, the lowest since such figures were first gathered in 1948. Calls from homeless youth to the National Runaway Switchboard increased 5 percent since 2011, 50 percent since 2009, and 80 percent since 2002.

It takes courage or desperation to swallow enough fear, pride, and adolescent invincibility to come through the doors of one of Covenant House's shelters. The young people are a varied group, but they have all been sorely tested. Only 41 percent have a high school diploma. In a recent study of five representative shelters by the Covenant House Institute, the organization's research arm, 40 percent of the kids had been in foster care or another institutional setting, 38 percent had experienced physical abuse, and 40 percent of the teenage girls and young women had been sexually abused. Almost 80 percent of the young people were unemployed, 63 percent lacked health insurance, and more than a quarter had been hospitalized for depression, anxiety, or other mental health issues. More than half came from a family where someone used drugs regularly. Many of the kids have been told, over and over until it echoes in their heads like a voice of their own, that they are worthless and will never amount to anything.

Yet there is one main reason most of them have no place to stay: their parents or guardians left them, discarded them, or abused them, physically, sexually, and/or emotionally, further stacking the odds against them. Based on decades of research, the U.S. Centers for Disease Control and Prevention and Kaiser Permanente's Health Appraisal Clinic in San Diego describe nine adverse childhood experiences that harm young people's long-term health and well-being, including emotional or physical neglect; losing a parent; physical, sexual, or emotional abuse; witnessing violence against their mother; and having a family member who is incarcerated, mentally ill, or an addict. Young people who have had such experiences have greater chances of becoming teen parents, being hospitalized for a mental disorder, and suffering from a broad variety of physical problems later in life, including miscarriage, stroke, and heart disease. The damage caused by such childhood experiences is cumulative, with the risk of health problems and heartache in adulthood increasing with each additional childhood hardship. Most of the young people in this book have survived at least five such difficult events, *through no fault of their own.*

Despite all of the challenges and dangers they have faced, many homeless youth yearn for home and for their families. Their homing instinct can be the animating force in their lives, a call from deep within the cells, leading them backward, sometimes at their peril. It is part of the psychology of children to blame themselves for whatever goes wrong in their families and to want to repair it. That desire, no matter how irrational, can drive a young person to desperate and at times dangerous feats. Paulie's family disintegrated around him when he turned thirteen, but he chased its vestiges on long bus rides, across time zones and national boundaries. Creionna's home was so dreary and loveless that she escaped, before she was quite ready, to build a family of her own. Muriel blamed herself for her father's departure from her family and sought home in the center of a loveless human trafficking ring.

Covenant House and youth shelters across North and Central America can become a bridge forward for young people who have nowhere to go. Our message to kids: even if you can't go home again, because your parents are missing or dead or abusive or in jail or hate you for who you are, you are still valuable and special and deserve safe shelter. You still have the right to a future. We open our doors, and we promise safety. We want to help you find stability, and we want you to pursue your dreams. We want you to rise up and move ahead, guided by your own hopes.

Even more important, we promise absolute respect and unconditional love. And with that love comes a lesson too few have learned: you are amazing. You are just as God made you. You are lovable, and, with any luck, you will come to understand and share in our love for you.

From seeing the sad weariness in the young people who need shelter, our greatest hope is to reduce sharply the number of kids experiencing homelessness each year. Many forces contribute to the growing stream of young faces at our doors and the doors of other shelters. This book considers them and highlights promising ways to address each one.

If we could improve the child welfare system, safely reducing the number of young people taken from their homes and put into foster care settings, there may be fewer kids turning into adults without a family to call their own, and fewer homeless young adults soon afterward.

As of 2010, about twenty-eight thousand young people turned eighteen in foster care each year and were left to fend for themselves. (If there were ever a figure to prove that government can never love a child the way a family can, this is it.) In one study, more than a fifth of them became homeless within a year of leaving foster care. The odds worsen as young people grow older—in one study, 37 percent of former foster children had been homeless by age twenty-four. If there were fewer kids in foster care, fewer aging out without families, and more help available for those who do, the knocks on our doors would decrease sharply.

If young people with mental illnesses and addictions could be treated consistently, using the best available therapies, fewer would end up in trouble at home and in school, and fewer would require shelter. Many of the kids we serve have been diagnosed with a mental health issue, often depression or anxiety, a natural result of living with abusive families or on the streets. Too often, they seek solace from their troubles in drugs or alcohol, which only damages them further.

If we could reduce homophobia, making it easier for parents to understand and support their children, regardless of sexual orientation, there would be fewer young people pushed to the streets and to the shelter door. Solutions are rarely simple, but if we could encourage more parents to substitute compassion for judgment, we would stem the tide of kids shamed out of their homes into the dark abandon of street life.

Likewise, if we could reduce the chances that pimps pick up runaway and throwaway kids and send them out to be raped repeatedly for someone else's profit, and if we could help create more safe havens for young people trying to break free of prostitution, we would see fewer sexually exploited young people coming into the shelters. If we could make it even half as taboo to buy and sell kids for sex as it is to buy and smoke cigarettes, we would make huge inroads against human trafficking.

And if we could provide mentors to young people whose parents have died or gone missing, if we could develop ways to encourage young fathers to stay with their children for decades, instead of weeks, we would better tap into the resilience of young people who might otherwise give in to despair or become parents before they are old enough to vote.

Though ambitious, none of these steps is impossible. The causes of youth homelessness are complex and interrelated but not overwhelming. We know what they are, and we know how to address them. There are concrete and helpful steps you can take, today, even without leaving your home. Small steps, large steps, steps to help reduce the number of scared, tired, and beaten-down kids who have nowhere to go but a shelter.

Many of the young people we meet have formidable powers of persistence and deep wells of strength. The counselors at Covenant House know that they can't erase all the pains of childhood, but they can provide a safe, caring place for kids to exhale and to plan their next steps. The shelters act as a greenhouse in a way, providing conditions conducive to growth and transformation. How can a young person find a job with dirty clothes, an empty stomach, and a huge sleep deficit? How can someone pass a school exam when he or she hasn't had a shower in weeks and doesn't have books or a quiet place for studying? How can a new mother get any rest in a home where she feels her baby is unsafe? The shelters meet basic needs, so that the young people staying there can focus on their higher goals. And while they are with us, they can see that they are not alone. They no longer need to feel isolated, as if they are the only ones who have been beaten, bullied, or troubled by secrets.

Each day, scores of kids walk into Covenant Houses across the Americas for the first time. More than half say they have gone at least a week without a nutritious meal. They get what they need immediately: a shower, food, clothes, a warm bed, and medical care, if they require it—more than a third do. Then, Covenant House has expectations of the kids. Once they're settled in, it's time for them to make a plan. The staff promises to help them, and the kids promise to help themselves—that's the covenant.

They discuss with trained counselors the causes of their home-lessness, their most critical needs, and the steps they will take to meet them. Is it safe to be reunited with their immediate families, or could they live with other relatives? What kind of jobs do they need? Do they want to finish high school or go to college? Do they need child care, substance abuse counseling, or job skills? Do they hope to support themselves on their own?

Preparing young people for jobs is part of Covenant House's most practical and important work. In most Covenant House programs, for example, young people can take a class on how to find, apply for, and keep a job in a competitive market. They can use computers to research leads and write resumes, and staff and volunteers coach them for job interviews. Once the young people have found jobs, Covenant House staff keeps in touch with their employers, to help iron out any problems or disagreements that could put those positions at risk.

Some of our shelters also provide training in skills that are in high demand. Covenant House in New York City has a six-month training course for young people to become state-certified nurses' aides. The shelter also offers ways for young people to earn their food handlers' licenses, by working and training in the dining room. In addition, residents work in the shelter's housekeeping and security departments and can obtain a certification in security and fire safety in a two-week training program.

Covenant House in St. Louis employs young people who live at the shelter to clean up two neighborhoods in the city, which gives them up to six months of real-life job experience. And a new program at an innovative café has provided jobs for young people at the shelter. Panera Cares, a restaurant created by Panera Bread Company founder Ronald M. Shaich that offers meals to patrons on a pay-as-you-can basis, gave internships to three Covenant House residents, with the hope of providing them with jobs and the potential for advancement in the company. Panera chose young people who had struggled with gaining and maintaining employment and trained them in customer service, time management, and handling conflict in the workplace. After completing the ten-week unpaid internships, all three received a stipend and were hired at local Panera locations.

The shelters' programs make a difference in young people's lives. A 2000 study by the Menninger Foundation found that in New York, almost two-thirds of the residents of Covenant House achieved at least one major goal while they lived there. A full 70 percent landed in stable housing six months after leaving the shelter. Although only 10 percent of the young people were employed when they came to Covenant House, that more than quadrupled six months after they left. Although 28 percent were severely depressed when they arrived, that rate fell by more than half, six months after they left. In both New York and California, the study found that the longer a young person stayed at Covenant House, the better he or she fared six months later. For example, four out of five of the young people who stayed for about two months were working or in school when they left. (That's true for young people whose only alternative to a shelter is the streets; longer stays in emergency shelters for children in the foster care system can often have a detrimental

effect if the youngsters are missing the chance to live in a nurturing home.)

Covenant House is not an anything-goes program. Young people can be asked to leave temporarily for serious fighting or being
under the influence of drugs or alcohol or for repeatedly failing to
follow their plans. But the kids know that our doors remain open,
and when former residents return, we stand ready to coach them
and to cheer for them, starting all over again, if necessary.

To complete the book, we conducted more than 175 interviews and
visited more than 25 cities across North America, talking to people
involved with these young lives: parents, foster parents, uncles and
aunts, siblings, coaches, mentors, and, at Covenant House, main-
tenance workers, cooks, counselors, and executive directors. We
also talked to dozens of experts on the issues that force children out
of their homes. We collected and reviewed thousands of documents, including foster care files, criminal records, report cards,
transcripts, and contemporaneous letters and journals.

For their privacy and protection, we refer to the young people,
their family members, and other acquaintances by pseudonyms.
When they were clearly identifiable in the schools or other institutions where they studied or worked, the names of those institutions
have been changed as well. In the case of Paulie, a handful of
potentially identifying details have been altered, none of which
change the truth of his experiences. No other names, dates, or
information has been changed.

We hope the stories that follow, taken together, will help reveal
the heart and the face of homeless youth across Canada and the
United States and the abundant generosity of adults who made a
difference for them. The portraits relay the toughness of the times,
the resilience of homeless young people, and the life-affirming acts
of kindness from adults who surround them with love and hope.

The young people and many of their allies allowed us into their lives in an extraordinary way, giving us hundreds of hours of their time, hashing over in detail some of their most difficult experiences. We approach the young people as their advocates, but in order to understand the extent of their ultimate achievements, we have not shied away from presenting their occasional shortcomings and the challenges of those who aspired to help them.

As parents ourselves, we understand that none of these kids deserved to suffer as they did. The book recalls profound and sometimes serial childhood maltreatment, and during our research, we have felt rage and, eventually, some compassion toward the adults who hurt the six young people, leaving grievous scars. We have also felt joy at the small, sometimes anonymous kindnesses that helped pull the kids through—the seeming bit players who made significant differences in their lives. They all raised small lanterns that helped the kids follow a safer path. Look around in your life to see if you, too, can find a young person who needs nothing more than encouragement, and odds are you can.

It is hopeful work, to help someone at the crossroads take concrete steps toward a fulfilling future, away from the specter of chronic homelessness, of growing old—or dying young—on the streets. At Covenant House, the staff often feels outmatched by the depths of young people's suffering and need. We are an imperfect crew, struggling against forces bigger and older than us: poverty, inequality, and violence, among others.

Yet for forty years, one thing has remained true at Covenant House: we sit ringside for some of the most miraculous and unlikely transformations of the human spirit. To be sure, there's room for many more to join in this hopeful movement, and to help.

1

A Son Walks Alone
Paulie's Story

Soon after Paulie was born, the fates seemed to have it in for him, pulling him from loved ones, beating him up, tearing his families apart, sending him demon after demon to wrestle. When we think of him as a newborn, we imagine softer landings for him. But our respect for Paulie, the teenager, the young man, the champion kickboxer, the cook who shares his skills, is boundless.

Thirteen-year-old Paulie Robbins sat up in bed, jolted awake by the shaking ground and the bouncing coins on his nightstand. It was yet another tremor in Palmer, Alaska, this one magnitude 4.0, enough to wake him at nearly one thirty one morning in December 1997. He rubbed his face groggily. In disorienting moments like this, he wished his father were home to be the man of the house. But Hank, a crab fisherman, was out on the Bering Sea, leaving Paulie's mother, Tiffany, alone with Paulie and his nine-year-old sister, Casey, in their trailer.

Hank's weeks away from them were a mixed blessing. He could be boisterous and lively, bringing the kids to garage sales in search of discarded treasures. He filled the shed he had built adjacent to the family's trailer with bargain tools and used them to repair toasters, bicycles, lamps, door hinges, anything that needed fixing. In the summertime, Hank took the kids camping and fishing, trolling for salmon on the Kenai River. An experienced angler, he taught them how to catch rainbow trout on Skilak Lake, baiting their gang hooks with worms as they faced the glacier at the head of the basin. Indoors, though, Hank was another man entirely. His angry, violent outbursts regularly left Tiffany or the kids crumpled in tears.

Paulie still flinched recalling an afternoon many years earlier, when during a disagreement between his parents that escalated into a brawl, Tiffany fell to the carpet with a bloody nose, and Paulie, just six, rose to defend her. But his father pinned him against the wall in front of the dining cabinet, his hand around his son's throat. Then, suddenly, he dropped Paulie and left the room, returning moments later with a gun. Paulie thought, "Oh my God, he is going to kill me." But Hank did not point the gun at Paulie, nor at Tiffany. Instead, he put the barrel in his own mouth and forced Paulie to put his small finger on the trigger.

"It's time for you to make the decision what you're going to do for the rest of your life," Hank hollered into Paulie's face. The boy cried, silently. Tiffany, who had wet herself from anxiety, vomited. *I should do something*, she thought, but she was frozen. Eventually, Hank scoffed at Paulie for refusing to shoot, then left the trailer in a rage.

The violence accelerated, and Tiffany descended into depression as their seventeen-year marriage wore on. A sour melancholy, beyond what's common during the long, dark Alaskan winters, often paralyzed her. She slept away hours of the day, escaping via a mixture of antidepressants and pain medication prescribed for recurring back problems. Her frizzy reddish-brown hair splayed across her face as she dozed in the dark wood-paneled living room, sometimes leaving a dangling lit cigarette for Paulie or Casey to douse.

Paulie stood up and glanced at Casey asleep in the top bunk. He shadowboxed a bit near his sister's head, thinking about how his father would cheer from the stands during his Pop Warner football games. He sometimes felt more exhilaration from that sound than from victory on the football field. Paulie cherished that fleeting feeling, the thrill of seeing his father beam with pride, video camera in hand, his whole family together and happy.

Yet the last football season had ended badly for Paulie, and he was eager to prove himself again to his father. He had steamed through a fantastic fall, throwing dozens of touchdowns. His Bruins were undefeated, 8–0, coming into the playoffs against the rival Wolverines.

The Bruins went ahead early in the game, but the score tightened as the clock ticked down, and with just minutes to go in the fourth quarter, Paulie could not find an open receiver downfield. He took matters into his own hands and ran out of the pocket for the end zone. He peeled past the defensive line, and with only a free safety to beat, he raced to the goal line. The defender dove at Paulie's heels, tripping him up a few yards shy of the end zone, and Paulie, thrown off balance, leaped with the ball to try to score. But his arm hit the turf hard and bent fully backward, pulverized. Paulie held onto the ball, short of the touchdown. The crowd rose, hushed, as his coach and his mother raced onto the field. Sobbing and unable to talk, he limped to the sidelines, passing his father, who repeatedly asked what was wrong.

Tiffany brushed Hank away and led Paulie to a chair. He hunched over in severe pain, oblivious to his surroundings until he felt a sudden jerk as Hank's hand reached down and pulled his injured arm.

"Quit your bawling," he said, cursing. "Tell me what happened or I'm taking your whiny little ass home!"

Paulie walked to the car behind his family, his head bowed, his arm in excruciating pain. Casey was already in the backseat, and

Tiffany was in the front passenger seat, nursing a new welt on her eye. Paulie asked her what happened, and she insisted it was nothing, that she had tripped and fallen. They rode in silence to the hospital, where X-rays showed Paulie had fractured his humerus bone. The doctor reset it and applied a cast that ended Paulie's football season and the family's outings for the year. Hank's video recorder went into storage. The Bruins buckled a few weeks later in the championship game, with their star quarterback sitting on the sidelines.

Paulie was devastated, and Tiffany tried in the immediate aftermath to boost his spirits and remind him that the setback was temporary. Paulie still remembers with a grin how she looked him in the eyes each morning and encouraged him, "You are going to grow up and be something special, Paulie. You're not like everybody else. You've been given a gift." For her part, Tiffany hoped those words would inoculate him against the loss of his football season and other rough punches to come.

That early morning after the shaking of the ground woke him, he faked one more hit in Casey's direction and climbed back in bed, ready to sleep again. *At least Mom's still here,* he thought as he drifted off to sleep.

Not long after the earthquake, Tiffany obtained a new antidepressant prescription from her doctor, and as the drugs started working, she took stock of her contentious marriage, realizing she'd had enough. She collected her children around the kitchen table one morning and delivered two strong aftershocks: she did not intend to let Hank back into the trailer when he returned, and she had invited a man named Ben, whom she had met online, to visit them for Christmas. She described what a nice man Ben was and how he lived south of them in Alberta. It was plain to Paulie that Ben was not just any visitor—Paulie had watched Tiffany feverishly typing for hours at a time online. To get her attention, he sometimes crouched next to the screen, facing her, close enough to smell the nicotine on her breath, but she stayed thousands of miles away, her eyes obscured by the reflection of the monitor on her large glasses. Looking to catch his mother's glance, he instead found in her glasses a wall of backward type.

Now he saw a new liveliness in her eyes, as she encouraged the kids not to worry about this new visitor. And, she added, they didn't have to call him "dad" if they didn't want to.

When Ben arrived, Paulie did not call him dad or anything remotely like it. Ben was nothing like his father. Hank was stocky and strong; Ben was lean and wiry. Paulie carefully danced around him, eyeing him suspiciously, declining offers of kindness and assistance.

Ben seemed to sweep into their lives seamlessly, helping with the chores, wrapping Christmas presents, and sleeping with Tiffany in Hank's bed. It was unreal, and although Tiffany seemed happier than Paulie had ever seen her, he knew it could not last. He dropped to the lower bunk at night, aware that just a few feet away, his mother was enmeshed with her new boyfriend, while his father planned his return. He waited, watching the foundation of their family teetering. Something had to give.

Sure enough, it did. A few days later, Ben's estranged wife killed herself in their home in Alberta. Paulie couldn't quite make out the whispering between Ben and his mother during the next two days, but he listened intently, in anger and shock, when Tiffany sat the kids down once again and explained that Ben needed her help in Canada. She and Ben would be leaving together after Christmas. She described it as a fast trip, just to take care of a few things, and pledged they would return to the kids in a week. She sent Paulie and his sister to live with different friends. Paulie left home a day before his fourteenth birthday with some clothes, socks, and underwear hastily packed into a small duffle bag.

After a week, however, Tiffany sent word that Ben could not come back to Alaska, having previously overstayed his visa in the United States. Plus, Ben had his hands full in Canada, trying to win two of his four children back from foster care and removing his late wife's belongings from their home. Tiffany had to decide whether to return to Alaska alone or stay with Ben and try to arrange for the kids to join her in Alberta down the road. It was an easy choice for her. Alaska held mostly bad memories for Tiffany, but with Ben, she had found an ease and a peace she could not, would not, relinquish. She promised to apply for a student visa to allow Paulie to join her in Alberta, and she arranged for him to move in with one of her friends in the meantime. When Hank returned from crab fishing, he found his trailer empty, his family gone. He picked up Paulie and Casey and, in a rage, forced them to choose where they would live. Neither was eager to answer, but when repeatedly pressed, Casey chose Hank and Paulie chose Tiffany. His mother was the weaker of the two, and Paulie worried about her. Hank erupted, and nothing was ever the same again.

Until Paulie could move to Canada, he stayed with a girlfriend of Tiffany's, who gave him more freedom than he had ever experienced. It was intoxicating. The woman's son, more than ten years older than Paulie, roamed with a carefree tribe of twentysomethings, and Paulie, often unsupervised, lost weekends and eventually schooldays to cocaine and cribbage marathons, poker tournaments, and beer pong. He soon began to experiment with marijuana and other drugs, all readily available. As the weeks turned into months and the temperatures climbed enough for the spring break-up to begin, Paulie's attendance at school fell off, and he became edgy and unhappy about the long wait to rejoin what was left of his family. Just a week before his last day of eighth grade, he attacked the bully from gym class, who had been taunting him about his missing mother for much of the winter. Paulie left the boy's face bloody and swollen, with his bottom lip split wide open. During middle school, Paulie had been a scrappy kid, encouraged by his father to fend for himself, but now he felt out of control, and the school agreed, expelling him.

Early that summer, after six months away, Tiffany finally sent a ticket for Paulie to join her and Ben in Alberta. When Paulie arrived at their home, he could see that Tiffany had settled into her new life without looking back. Ben's older child in the house, a six-year-old boy with autism, was a handful, but he and his four-year-old sister looked to Tiffany as their mother. And she embraced the role, announcing to Paulie within minutes of seeing him that she and Ben planned to marry soon.

Paulie didn't feel like he fit in. He continued to experiment with different drugs—downers, Ecstasy, cocaine—in larger doses, occasionally breaking into his mother's room to steal her pot. Ben tried to encourage him to attend high school in Calgary, and Paulie seemed momentarily to hit his stride when the football coach discovered his strong arm and gave him a spot on the team, but it was not nearly as much fun as it had been up north. He missed his teammates, he missed his family cheering on the sidelines, and he missed home.

He even missed Tiffany, even though she was right there in front of him. He loved her, and he knew she loved him in her way, but he felt like a spectator or a houseguest in her new family, not a son. The painkillers Tiffany had become increasingly reliant on muddled her mind and pushed her further away from him. Paulie eventually quit school, idling away most of the day, sometimes watching the children or listening to Tiffany's wedding plans. When the big day arrived, he put on his most ardent smile and sat to the right of his mother, watching her marry Ben in the very spot in their living room where Ben's late wife had died one year earlier.

Over time, Paulie started returning home at odd hours of the night, addled, incoherent, pale. New blond streaks lined his jet black hair, and he grew a stubby goatee, making him look older than his fifteen years. He ignored curfews, and Tiffany had a hard time keeping track of him.

She woke him one morning in his makeshift basement bedroom and discovered piles of shoplifted clothes. Paulie was planning to wear some and sell some for drug money. It was more than Tiffany could bear. She was not yet a Canadian citizen and worried that officials would discover the theft and punish her, perhaps forcing her to leave the country and her life with Ben.

She telephoned the authorities, turned Paulie in, and watched the police handcuff him and take him away. Paulie headed to a group home for delinquent youth. Before long, he was roaming Calgary, intermittently sleeping at Ben and Tiffany's house or on the streets, watching the hookers and the drug addicts. This was no life, he thought. He had a better shot back in the 907 area code—friends, a sister, even his estranged father. Maybe he could reconstruct some semblance of a home back there, and, in any event, it was clear to him, at the age of fifteen, that he had run his course with his mother and her new family.

Tiffany warned him not to go back to Hank in Alaska, predicting they would not get along, but when she could not persuade him, she handed him a creased and faded sheet of yellowed loose-leaf paper. "This is from your mother," she said, "your biological mother."

Paulie stopped short, speechless. He knew he had been adopted, but he had no idea his birth mother had left him a note. When he was eleven or twelve, Paulie's parents had told him his birth mother, who they said was a teenage runaway, had abandoned him in a shed in the Alaskan countryside as an infant. How could he have a letter from her now, fifteen years later? He opened the letter immediately and read its contents. His correspondent, homeless and then just seventeen, said she knew he wouldn't understand why she had chosen to surrender him, but hoped he might one day forgive her. And then, as only a mother can know, especially a young mother who for two years struggled to keep him safe and make ends meet, she explained:

> I didn't do this because I don't love you or want you. I did this because I would much rather die than see you be deprived of a father, proper upbringing, and happiness, for you are my world . . . I don't expect you to love me but I would love to meet you and see if you are well and happy . . . I love you my son. Please forgive me. Love you always, Frankie Sandmeyer

Reeling, Paulie put the note in his pocket and headed back to Anchorage, asking Hank if he could stay at the trailer. As Tiffany predicted, his arrival ignited a powder keg. Paulie and Hank fought constantly from the start. Hank was bigger and stronger than Paulie, and he had no tolerance for his son's drug use, his stealing, his flouting curfews. Their shouting matches routinely turned violent, and one in particular shook Paulie to his foundation.

Although he had been considered an eleventh grader in Canada, his Alaska high school put him back in ninth grade, and he cut a lot of school. When Hank caught him, he gave Paulie one of the worst beatings of his life—pulling his hair, kicking him, throwing him against the refrigerator, nearly breaking a table over him. Then he drove Paulie to school. During the ride, Hank cried his eyes out, saying how much he loved Paulie and wanted to be his friend. Dazed, still bleeding, Paulie sat motionless, wondering what love is.

A week or so after that fight, he called his football coach and said he wouldn't be playing on the team anymore, as he was leaving home. He left Hank's, empty-handed, and wandered the cold, dark streets of their northern town.

Paulie continued to become more involved with drugs, especially Ecstasy, a stimulant and low-level hallucinogen, stealing from local retailers so he could buy more pills. After he was arrested for shoplifting at a local store, Paulie tried to crash with his best friend, begging his friend's mother to hide him. But she knew Paulie had a juvenile record and was expected to report in regularly to a probation officer. She called the cops, who brought him to Covenant House in Anchorage, the only shelter for homeless and runaway teenagers in Alaska's largest city. Housed in the former downtown YMCA, the shelter was an unremarkable brick building that once had one of the city's only community pools. Covenant House had filled in the pool and converted the space into a living room for the city's destitute young people. Paulie could hardly believe he had become one of them.

Arriving at Covenant House

Mildred Mack was working an overnight shift when she first saw Paulie walk through the front door of the shelter. She had started at Covenant House six years earlier, in 1993, after the breakup of her nearly twenty-year marriage. She had loyally supported her ex-husband's army career, moving with him from Kansas to Hawaii to Georgia, uprooting their son and daughter each time, and finally arriving in Alaska. After the divorce she was faced with raising two teenagers on her own.

Mildred was hard to miss, one of the few African American faces in a city that is more than 70 percent white. She was older than the rest of the shelter staff—well into her fifties, with wavy brown hair combed forward and high cheekbones that cradled inquiring, wide eyes. By most accounts, she was no-nonsense, demanding, and relentless, qualities that had helped her put her children's lives back together after the divorce, when all she really wanted to do was cry herself to sleep. She had found a way to force a smile and put food on the table, with no time for self-pity, hers or anyone else's. It was Paulie's terrible misfortune, he would soon think, to have Mildred Mack as his primary counselor.

When Paulie first arrived at Covenant House, it was obvious he needed sleep, a warm shower, and food. He came exhausted, having couch-surfed from one friend's home to another, sometimes with their parents' knowledge, other times sneaking inside after they went to bed. He spent a few nights walking the streets, bundled against the freezing temperatures, tired, and hungry. His body was just run down. The staff at Covenant House called local child welfare authorities to report Paulie's allegations of physical abuse, and called Hank to notify him of Paulie's presence at the shelter and request some clothes, but Hank refused. The next day, Paulie called Hank directly. Crying, he asked his father for his clothes, but Hank rebuffed him and fumed that Paulie was just avoiding reality by not getting help for his drug problem.

"Why don't you come home and stand up to me like a man?" Hank said.

"I will when I'm not a toothpick," Paulie responded, "when I can stand up to you without getting beat up."

After letting him rest a few days, Mildred expected more from him. He needed counseling, she was certain. He talked longingly of a birth mother he had never met and denied having a drug problem. He seethed about feelings of abandonment, Hank's beatings, and the many reasons he could not live with either parent, unloading story after story like a seasoned raconteur, but he was stymied by the simplest follow-up question: "What do you want to do about this?"

Mildred believed that Paulie needed to become serious about school, gather his important papers, and look for a part-time job. He had not finished one year of high school, and the longer he waited, the tougher it would be to earn his diploma. Without that, his prospects for finding his way off the streets would be much slimmer.

Paulie resisted and dawdled, complaining that neither parent had his birth certificate, so he couldn't go to school or work. He lounged on the shelter's couches and overslept, avoiding Mildred whenever possible. When she found him, she put him to work and peppered him with questions about his plans. Had he seen the social worker? Had he gotten his social security card? Did he go to school? And she was firm with him about the curfew that Paulie creatively attempted to flout, citing all manner of natural disasters and public transportation calamities.

He insisted that he needed a break. Mildred told him Covenant House *was* his break. He felt he needed a friend, but Mildred said she wasn't his buddy. She had a higher purpose in his life; she believed he could move himself forward—she could see it in him, plain as day.

Actually, she saw equal parts resilience and rage. She could tell Paulie had promise, but he was shiftless, simmering with anger, and unsure of himself. He peppered the conversations with Mildred with unsolicited non sequiturs: "I'm not a bad person," "I think my mother really wants me to be with her but she has a lot going on in Canada right now," "I really don't deserve to get beat up all the time," "I think I have some good qualities." She listened and probed during dozens of conversations. She tried to affirm and encourage him, but she knew that he was not trying to convince her or anyone else of his self-worth; he was trying to sort it out for himself.

As suddenly as he had arrived at the shelter, Paulie left, AWOL one night without so much as a good-bye. Mildred had seen it coming for days. Moments after Paulie left the shelter, Tiffany returned the staff's call of several days prior. She told them she was Paulie's official guardian and assured them "if Paulie made allegations of abuse against Hank, they are true." When staff advised her of the pending child abuse investigation, she ended the call by pledging to dial the state child welfare agency, but the allegation against Hank had been dismissed for lack of evidence by the time Tiffany called.

He went back to Hank's trailer, where Hank beat him worse than Paulie could ever recall, zip tying his thumbs behind his back and throwing him into the car. Before they went into the probation office, Hank cut the ties and hauled Paulie across the parking lot. Hank told the probation officer that he could not handle Paulie any longer. Together, Hank and the probation officer agreed to send Paulie for an assessment at a local psychiatric hospital, then to a drug rehabilitation center in Idaho, for two years. Paulie and another boy attempted to escape after only two months. They were caught and locked in a juvenile jail for a month.

Idaho officials contacted Tiffany and agreed to bus Paulie to the border of British Columbia from the detention center after his stint ended. But when Paulie stepped off the bus at the border crossing in the dead of winter, Tiffany was unable to meet him; she lacked the necessary immigration documents. She wept through the phone, urging Paulie to wait on the Idaho side of the border until she could develop a plan. It was getting late. Paulie lay down on the curb and put his jacket over his legs to keep warm. When that failed, he walked over to the visitors' center bathroom to warm himself with the hand dryers, making four or five trips throughout the night.

The next evening, Tiffany finally appeared in a friend's car and told Paulie to hop inside. They drove around looking for a less traveled route into Canada and found one where the agent waved them right in. Paulie entered Canada illegally that night, joining Ben, Tiffany, and the children just as they were preparing to relocate to Ontario, on Ben's whim. On the way east, they slept in their station wagon, stuffed with their pets and all of their possessions.

As they settled into their new home, Paulie slowly realized that Tiffany had become a prescription pill junkie. She'd found a new doctor in Ontario right away, one who gave her Oxycontin and Valium. She was hooked almost immediately and took Ben down with her. Virtually comatose during the day, Tiffany let cigarettes burn holes on the couch, the recliner, and eventually her own knees and legs. Mired in addiction, she and Ben faded away, and life unfolded in slow motion, painkillers thickening the couple's words and movements. Paulie introduced his mom to a local drug dealer, and they returned to the house and took morphine pills together, the boundaries between mother and son eroding further and further. Paulie spent less and less time at home, running away frequently, taking up with local truants, petty thieves, and drug couriers.

In a few months, he returned to the streets of Anchorage, tiring of Tiffany's addiction but knowing Hank's place was no longer an option. He felt unnerved by an abiding sense of not belonging that he could not overcome. Tiffany had tried to love him as best she could. Paulie did not blame her for failing to protect him from Hank's fists, though Tiffany blamed herself. Looking back on Paulie's childhood, from the safety and security of her new life in Canada, Tiffany indicted herself for not standing up to Hank more. During all of those years in the trailer, she was a wreck. She threw up virtually every day for a decade, a jumble of depression and dread. She believed that if she dared intervene on behalf of the kids, Hank would kill her. Yet later, away from Hank, she could not shake an overwhelming sense of remorse.

It was not all Hank's fault, either, Paulie knew. Hank had encouraged Paulie to share some of his core passions: fighting, fishing, and football. That was how a man like Hank expressed affection. Some days, Paulie felt that his father just suffered an accursed temper that made him impossible to live with, but the problem was bigger than that.

There was something wrong with them as a family. They didn't go together. The pieces did not fit. This was not about love, whatever that was; this was about connection. The older he got, the more distant Paulie felt from all of them. It was too easy to live apart from them, to say good-bye and not miss them deeply. He came to think of them as his rented family, and he did not belong to them or with them. Home was somewhere else, it had to be. He searched for it, yearning. The chase took him everywhere and nowhere, six months with Tiffany and Ben, six months with friends in Anchorage on the streets, a few months with a relative in the Lower 48, a chain of group homes, Covenant House, Anchorage's parks, the transit center, street corners, and benches.

Alaska's rave scene temporarily quenched Paulie's thirst, introducing him to a community of dance party and drug enthusiasts. Raves popped up across the city, starring turntable magicians who pushed the churning dance floor into all-night frenzies with a succession of fast-paced electronic songs and accompanying light shows. Paulie favored trance music, and he was attractive in that crowd, his piercing brown eyes suggesting sensitivity, his square jawline virility. The girls flocked to him. He spent countless nights spinning and swaying to the progression of thumping sounds spun by the rave's DJ ringmaster. The communal spirit of the dance floor filled him with a sense of belonging. He didn't have to ponder his lost home and family; the music invaded all of his senses. The bigger the space, the more dancers in his midst, sweating and moving in sync to the music, the better he felt.

In no time, he was drawn into a drug subculture among the ravers, centered on Ecstasy. Some called it the hug drug, because they claimed it helped them be more in touch with their feelings, thawing hearts and minds in the frozen north. But the side effects could be serious: depression and paranoia, not to mention involuntary teeth clenching, blurry vision, and increased heart rate.

Paulie peddled the green-and-blue tablets before and during raves and, for a while, made a life of it. He was sleeping on the streets or on friends' couches or bundling with other ravers in a shared hotel room or in Town Square Park, across from Covenant House. But Anchorage was freezing—the snow fell from late September to April, and in midwinter, the sun barely showed up. After ten-hour dances on a drug that caused a marked spike in body temperature, Paulie struggled to stay warm. When he became too cold and weary, he returned to Covenant House, and Mildred soon caught on to his pattern: first asking for help, then professing to change his life, followed by resistance, anger, and a quick exit. The steps refueled him for the next foray on the streets, but he never tackled the heartache and the substance abuse that continually kept him in bad straits. He missed his mother and felt deeply alone. The drugs took hold of him, and didn't let go.

He idled on the top level of the F Street mall, buying one soda and refilling it all day so no one would kick him out for loitering. He pinched food from the garbage and could find a coat, gloves, or fresh socks from Covenant House any time he wanted, whether he lived there or not. But he was decidedly not interested in the shelter's rules, least of all the ten o'clock curfew. He wanted liberty.

By the time he was seventeen, he had come to Covenant House eight times in nearly three years, and most times he'd leave in a huff, after complaining about Mildred "getting in my face." He was unwilling to return to school or study for his high school equivalency diploma (GED). He missed meals and counseling. When Mildred laid down the law and told him not to waste his days loitering downtown, he bristled, and the lure of the streets prevailed. The parties, the beer, the drugs, and, most of all, the freedom trumped Mildred's voice, Mildred's rules, Mildred's agenda for his life.

Most days, Paulie was glad for the dark, and there was a lot of it in Anchorage in the winter. It made it possible for him to hide, backing up into doorways, sleeping on or under benches, without feeling exposed. He didn't mind eating out of the trash cans as much as he minded being seen doing so. But the eighteen-hour winter nights were dangerous. Homeless people routinely freeze to death on the streets of Anchorage; some have been crushed to death when the dumpsters they sought shelter in were emptied into trash trucks.

In 2009, Covenant House Alaska and the Institute of Social and Economic Research at the University of Alaska, Anchorage, published results from a ten-year review of more than four thousand individual case files belonging to youth who sought shelter between 1999 and 2008. Like Paulie, 66 percent of those young people had not finished high school, and 40 percent of them had lived in a mental health residential program. Nearly one in three kids who came to Covenant House Alaska had spent time in foster care. Almost half of the girls and young women at the shelter were survivors of sexual assault, as were about 7 percent of the boys.

These hardships were not unique to children and youth in Alaska. In one of the largest-ever studies of homeless youth in New York City, researchers at Columbia University's Center for Homelessness Prevention Studies, in partnership with Covenant House Institute, reported in 2009 that almost half of the 444 homeless youth who sought shelter at Covenant House New York reported significant violence at home. One in five reported being beaten with an object. Thirty-five percent of the young people had spent time in foster care. The data paint a stark picture of the life-altering events that may drive children into unaccompanied homelessness: abuse, instability, emotional trauma.

Paulie had confronted all three, so he was far from alone. Deeply isolated, he sought solace in the music, the community, and the pills of his rave world. He often found buyers among them for the handful of Ecstasy pills he carried with him, selling on the down low in bathrooms or dark corners of the floor. Eventually, the police caught up with him, charging him with twenty-five felonies—one for each pill he delivered in an unusually big deal and three for the other pills he had on him when he was arrested. He spent three months in the McLaughlin Youth Center, Anchorage's juvenile jail. He was just three months shy of his eighteenth birthday. If he had been tried as an adult, he might still be in prison. At McLaughlin, he appeared depressed, in part because he was coming down from the Ecstasy. He had eaten sporadically on the streets, so he arrived at McLaughlin looking gaunt. His record of hospitalization and treatment left McLaughlin officials worried that he was a suicide risk, so they isolated him. He could feel himself bottoming out, squandering the days on his cot, crying, wondering what kind of life this was. He wanted to change.

When the news of Paulie's arrest reached her at Covenant House, Mildred felt sad but not surprised. *Maybe this is what he needs*, she thought.

After returning to Covenant House from McLaughlin, Paulie was unhappy to find Mildred still there. She occasionally heard him grumbling about her, and she chalked it up to a play for sympathy. She was not out to win any popularity contests with the kids, and if she tried, she would lose badly. She did not hug or purr or sweet talk, and even if she did, she was sure those were not the things Paulie needed. He did not need another friend. Mildred watched him intensely, like an eagle attending its speckled eggs high above the arctic wilderness, trying to figure out what it was he needed most.

"Why can't you just leave me alone?" he pleaded one afternoon, sprawled across the couch, having failed to go to school yet

again. He had repeatedly told her about the humiliations of showing up with mismatched outfits from the shelter's clothing room.
Had she even been listening to him?

"These chores you should be doing, Paulie, one day they're
going to help you. You're going to go to work and have a good work
ethic, you know?"

"I am sick and tired of you with this tough love bull. Just leave
me alone!" he hollered.

She bent down to face him and saw him trembling, his eyes
moist, searching as far away from her as he could. She looked
into those tired brown eyes and for the first time she had second
thoughts. Maybe this was not the way. Maybe Paulie needed most
to retreat into his shell, to rest, protect himself, and heal. Maybe
the beatings and the drugs and the end of his family had exacted too
great a toll, and he was not as resilient as she had estimated. If she
turned her focus away from him, perhaps in time he would overcome his hurt and inertia. She wanted to give in, to tell him it was
okay just to lie back down and relax. But her steely determination,
which had forced her out of bed and into the workforce, would not
let her do it. She prayed for God to give her the wisdom and grace
to know what to do with this boy. She stood silently and waited for
Paulie to do his chores, and she didn't leave the room until she saw
him reluctantly pick up a broom and start sweeping the hall.

After an especially tense day with Paulie, Mildred unleashed her
frustration at the afternoon staff meeting. "I don't know how to reach
this boy," she said, almost pleadingly, and stopped herself short, the
plaintive tone in her voice lingering. It was a rare display of disquiet
from Mildred, whom younger coworkers dubbed Miss Military for
the confidence, structure, and discipline she brought to her work.
Mildred excused herself from the circle and retreated to an office,
where, hidden behind a stack of boxes, she cried quietly.

Working at Covenant House is not for the faint of heart. It is a calling, not a paycheck. Any young person staying at the shelter who thinks you're doing it for the money will tell you so, immediately and often. Imagine being a residential adviser in a college dorm, struggling to bring order to a crowd of sleep-deprived, hormone-addled, and opinionated young people living away from home, some for the first time. Then subtract most of the high school diplomas and stable family histories, and add trauma to the mix and varying degrees of loneliness, anxiety, and stress. Then put everyone in crisis, perhaps with fresh wounds from fights with family or friends or pimps or recent abandonment by foster care. Add a handful of mental illnesses and addictions, the panic of having no permanent address, and try to make sure everyone gets along enough and keeps quiet enough so that the others can rest. The goal is to do all of this with unconditional love and absolute respect. The work can take its toll.

Mildred went to find her long-time confidante and supervisor, Connie Morgan, a veteran of the shelter's first days in Anchorage. Connie originally hailed from Olive Hill, Kentucky, population seventeen hundred. That small town taught her to prize community, and her folksy, Southern amiability won friends readily, including native residents of the icy northern tundra of Alaska, where she had followed her husband on assignment from the federal Indian Health Service in the mid-1980s. Her natural affability thawed the reserve of the Inupiats she met in Barrow, the northernmost American city, and helped land her a spot as one of Covenant House Alaska's first employees, charged with helping to build the Anchorage program and recruit the new shelter team.

Connie could see Mildred struggling with Paulie. He always seemed to teeter on the ledge, leaning toward decisions that could help him turn his life around before he dove back into street life, never dealing with the grief over losing his home that he wore like an extra layer of skin. Mildred increasingly believed it was not enough to keep him warm and safe for a couple weeks, then watch him go back into the flux. She wanted to pull him off the edge of the abyss before he fell, save him from the streets and the drugs, get him focused on the promise of his life. But she didn't know how.

She trusted that Connie might. Connie had worked with hundreds of homeless teenagers, many of whom had survived unspeakable violence, and Connie repeatedly told her that no kid was unreachable. But Paulie's life was upside-down. His father beat him, and they could barely be in the same room together. His mother had abandoned him on her way to a new life in Canada, then did drugs with him. All of this left Paulie pining for some mysterious birth mother who had supposedly left him for dead in a shed as a baby. Grownups had unwittingly trained this boy never to trust them.

Connie suspected that he was too smart and handsome for his own good. Paulie's considerable intelligence, good looks, and abundant charm kept him from the harshest consequences of the streets. Even after stints in juvenile jails in Canada, Idaho, and Alaska, Paulie had avoided the bottoming out that landed many young drug abusers on the road to recovery and many homeless, truant teenagers back to school.

"A lot of our work is like small steps," Connie said to Mildred. "And not everything is going to go well. We can't expect kids to come in here and have some earth-shattering experience. Paulie has been through the mill. He keeps coming back, yes? He trusts us more each time, right?" Then she sighed, and answered her own question. "Right."

Connie knew that Mildred thought she had to be strong and demanding for Paulie's sake, but it was mostly a well-rehearsed facade. Underneath Mildred's veneer of certitude and toughness dwelled a soft center, one she hesitated to reveal. She needed permission to experiment a bit.

"Try something different," Connie advised. "He expects you to lean into him. Try giving him some carrots. If he wants an extra hour on curfew, barter: give it to him if he enrolls in the diploma course."

It could not hurt to try, so Mildred did just that. And in a matter of days, Paulie started to earn the privileges he sought. Suddenly, carrots in hand, Mildred found it easier to lure him toward an education. She still insisted they meet every day and review his plans and accomplishments. When he was late, she waited for him. When he feigned ignorance of the scheduled meeting time, she sought him out, without exception. She was not letting go.

A few weeks later, Paulie approached her in the hallway of the shelter. She sensed he was coming to the end of his latest stay, because his attendance at meals had become less frequent and his requests for extended curfews more common. "Mildred, I never did anything to you. Why can't you just leave me alone?"

She looked at him with a faint smile. He just shook his head, shrugged, and walked away.

Covenant House had started out for Mildred as a job. She was working at the Salvation Army after her divorce but not earning enough. She had read an article in 1990 about Covenant House Alaska after it first opened, the piece prominently featuring Covenant House's then president, Sister Mary Rose McGeady, talking about how the shelter gave her a way to bring the values of her faith into her work. Mildred, a fellow Roman Catholic, applied for a part-time position on the evening shift. Soon it became more than a job, and she left the Salvation Army to join Covenant House full time.

She was inspired by the shelter's dynamic duo: the unfussy and accessible Connie and the spunky young executive director, Deirdre Cronin, a red-headed fireball with a heavy Queens accent. Deirdre had volunteered at Covenant House in New York City right out of college, as part of its Faith Community program, a corps of volunteers who dedicate a year of their lives to work at Covenant House sites in Anchorage, Atlantic City, Fort Lauderdale, and New York. Deirdre moved to Alaska after Sister Mary Rose offered her the chance to lead her own agency, albeit one far from her family and friends. Deirdre jumped at the opportunity; her enthusiasm for serving homeless youth reached from the pushed-out kids of Times Square to runaways from the most remote Native Alaskan villages, no matter what their faith.

"I am a fan of Jesus," she often declared to the staff matter-of-factly, "and while I never met him personally, I'm pretty sure he never said you have to pray in order to eat and have shelter. They're all our kids."

When Paulie resurfaced at Covenant House at the age of nineteen in 2003, still homeless, tired, and cold, both Deirdre and Connie encouraged Mildred. "Find his spark, Mildred. You can do this," Connie said. If Mildred was feeling uncertain about how to break through to Paulie this time, both Deirdre and Connie had confidence she would do so, and Mildred never let Paulie see her doubt.

Paulie told her he wanted to stop eating out of trash cans. She told him he had to stop using drugs and get his equivalency diploma, a job, and some savings. He didn't quite roll his eyes, but it was close. She admired his courage for coming back yet another time, but she wished he would check his adolescent swagger at the door.

Paulie told her he had received his diploma a few weeks ago, without having had to study much. Mildred was speechless at first, then put her hands on his shoulders and gave them a shake, beaming. He had his GED? It was a terrific omen, and it confirmed to her that he was naturally smart. After all, he had no formal education beyond a few months of the ninth grade, yet had passed the high school equivalency exam on the first try.

"All right, then!" she said.

He had to smile. Her voice, the one that had taken root in his head during the last year, had finally started making sense. He heard it on the streets, in a crowd, though she was nowhere in sight. Nothing had gone right for him when he followed the ravers, the drug pushers, and the other kids on the street, so for something different, he had started to listen to the voice of Mildred Mack. Maybe she really did care about him. He wanted to make the right decisions, the kind that Mildred had been encouraging, choices that would help him off the streets. He was tired of being a victim.

During the next several weeks, she saw him for the first time apply himself steadily at the shelter, tackling his chores without any lip, finding a part-time job, then another, saving his paychecks, and expressing an interest in Covenant House's Rights of Passage independent living program, which gives young people the skills they need to prosper on their own, while insisting that they work, budget, and save during their extended stays.

He began to engage in the life of the shelter, owning his substance abuse, sharing openly at youth meetings about his use of Ecstasy and the downward spiral it caused. He wanted to make drugs a thing of the past, and he attended Narcotics Anonymous meetings, eventually joining peer counselors in downtown Anchorage to encourage homeless youth to avoid drugs and leave street life behind. He signed up for the shelter's chess tournament and won handily. And he poured himself into the weekly Cov Poetry Slam, writing about the quest for family and acceptance, sharing his poems with staff and other young people.

> A Knight walks alone
> Looking for his sister
> Do you know where you are?

Calls the voice
"No"
Do you know who your father is?
"No"

Within a month—his longest stay at Covenant House until then—Paulie was accepted into Rights of Passage, and he planned to leave the crisis shelter for his new digs several blocks away. The morning before he left, Paulie invited Mildred to go for a walk. They bundled up and headed outside, passing the mural painted across the back of the building depicting a young person sitting on a trash can next to the words "Life on the Street Is a Dead End."

"Umm, I just want to say thanks for helping me. You got my ass in line. You never gave up on me."

She shook her head no and reminded him of the last time he had stayed there, when he asked her why she wouldn't leave him alone.

"Yeah," he said. "You didn't really say anything."

"I know, I know," she said, looking down, pausing. "Paulie, I wanted to say never. I'm never going to leave you alone, you know, because I believe in you."

He faced her and quietly responded, "Thanks, Mildred."

"Don't thank me, Paulie. I did for you what I did for my own."

"I'm kind of your own by now," he said.

"That you are," she said with a grin.

At Rights of Passage, Paulie, who logged a grand total of eleven stays with Covenant House, had his ups and downs like all of the kids. He worked at Arby's at the mall during the day and spent a lot of time imagining life with his birth mother, wondering where she was, if she was even still alive. He grew certain that he wanted to try to find her, but he didn't know where to begin. His birth records were sealed, and he had no idea what she looked like, whether she had changed her name, where she lived. It was a painful cul-de-sac, longing to find her, knowing he could not, then fantasizing about her once again. At night in bed, he unearthed her letter to him, rereading it repeatedly. *She wanted me*, he thought. *Out there, somewhere, my mother wanted me.*

When he was twenty-one, he moved downtown into an apartment with a friend for five months before finding his own place three blocks from a spare, underground kickboxing center. The owner encouraged Paulie to give kickboxing a try, and it felt right to him.

Paulie lost his first public bout, which he invited his father to watch, but when he talked to Hank afterward, it was as if Paulie had won in a knockout. Hank was electric, impressed by how strong and fast his son had become. It reminded Paulie of those Pop Warner games. Eight years later—too late, on so many counts—Paulie had won his father's esteem as a fighter.

As a boy, he had cared more about his father's reaction than about the play on the football field. But now, although Hank's enthusiasm pleased Paulie somewhat, it did not color his perception of the match. Paulie had lost, and he did not want to do that again. He threw himself into the rigors of the ring, training four to six hours a day, all day on the weekends, weightlifting to build muscle on his lean frame. He never wanted to be skinny, which is how he saw himself, and his new routine helped him grow stronger and feel better about himself.

The sport taught him about staying on his feet when all he wanted to do was lie down. He relished the chance to care, bleed, coach, and sweat with kids who thought only about kickboxing, not about drugs, not about sex, not about violence, just about the respect they had for each other and for the sport.

He woke at four or five in the morning to run, then started his workday, and afterward returned to the gym until it closed.

For hundreds of hours during the next eight months, he practiced footwork, reflexes, and the finesse and reach of his kicks. He couldn't count on his bulk, so he won by wearing down his opponent with careful strategy. Victory was contingent on being in top physical form, and he was.

For Paulie, fighting allowed for the physicality of a street brawl without the negative feelings directed at his adversary. Most of the kicks did not even hurt Paulie when they landed, blunted by surges of adrenaline. The real pain came later that night or the next morning when he awoke unable to move a bruised, stiff limb or two. He took as his motto "Pain is the greatest teacher, time is the ultimate healer, and heartbreak is the best motivator."

Kickboxing seemed to Paulie the first of his pursuits that gave him back exactly what he put in. The harder he trained, the better he became. He loved feeling in control. His childhood and adolescence had been chaos, making him feel weak and adrift for so long that he had never imagined a sense of autonomy that was not drug-fueled. The sport redeemed him, he believed that. He would not eat from a trash can or sleep on the street again. He would not beg or steal or let himself be attacked again. He gloried in the ring, winning ten straight matches after his first loss, and within eight months, he won a statewide championship bout in his weight class.

Kickboxing did not pay most of his bills, though, and he kept busy in a number of Anchorage's best restaurants, first as a waiter, then as a cook, sometimes as both. He had not been back to the shelter in several years, though it was not far off his usual path. Eventually, he decided to volunteer at a dinner for the kids of Covenant House. He just felt it was time to give back. Paulie arrived at the restaurant before six o'clock in the morning on the day of the dinner to start prepping for 120 hungry kids and staff members. Once the other volunteers began showing up, about one for every young person, he walked down to Covenant House to escort the kids through the snow, to the restaurant. They had no idea what was in store.

Flowers graced every table in the burnt-sienna dining room. The menu included vegetable crudités, salad, rosemary poultry and stuffing, gravy, two kinds of potatoes, baked veggies, and three desserts: a chocolate cream pie, pecan pie, and apple crisp. The kids were awestruck. The meal was like nothing they had ever seen or tasted before.

Paulie worked the tables in his white chef's uniform with the grace of a practiced waiter, but by the time he had talked to the third or fourth kid, a wave of melancholy struck him as he remembered life on the streets. Whether he looked left or right, each face was his, a dizzying room of Paulie Robbinses. He was surprised to discover how much a part of their struggle he still was, feeling so connected to them and separate from society at the same time.

THE COSTS OF NOT CARING

—Tina Kelley

Sometimes, the right solution solves fiscal problems, as well as human ones. Homelessness is expensive, and helping young homeless people find a firm footing keeps them from becoming older homeless people, with more costly, entrenched health problems and chronic needs. According to a 2009 report of homeless people in Los Angeles, those ages forty-six to sixty-five accrue five times the health-care costs of those under thirty.

I've often been dismayed by the waste in government-sponsored social service solutions. Remember when New York City used to spend up to three thousand dollars a month to put homeless families in dangerous welfare hotels, when the same amount would have more than covered rent in a decent apartment? Have you watched the costs of health care skyrocket, in part because preventive or routine care is not available, and poor people end up sicker or dead, when the emergency room is their only option?

It just makes sense to meet human needs before they become more acute. That's how Covenant House saves society millions of dollars, with its ability to provide thousands of young people with safe shelter, affordable health-care referrals, educational programs, and employment help. Rights of Passage, our transitional living program, costs less than fourteen thousand dollars per young person, for an average stay of seven months, compared to forty-seven thousand dollars per year to keep a kid in juvenile detention in California.

Yet beyond the dollar costs, consider the psychic ones. After spending a night in a cardboard box as part of Covenant House's Solidarity Sleep Out for homeless youth, I understood much more about the toll "sleeping rough" takes on the hearts and the heads of young people. The cold, the noise, the wind, the fear—I don't know how kids bear it. They become exhausted and, eventually, sick from the cold and the worries that keep them awake. Imagine trying to get a good night's sleep in a subway car, in a rat-infested park, or in a room with someone who trades a bed for the use of your body. Imagine waking up having to figure out the next semiacceptable place to stay!

There are small steps that each of us can take to save the lives of our kids. Mildred grabbed hold of Paulie and never let go during the course of five years, even as he drifted away from her, over and over again. It begins there—taking an interest. The government will never love children the way families must, and when families cannot or will not, the answer is in each of us to find the extraordinary in the next Paulie and help unleash his sacred potential.

Without some of these actions, the lives of homeless young people can take deeply dreary turns—for want of a nail, the kingdom is lost. I often wonder how kids without a home fare in cities without safe shelters. The waste of potential, in terms of human and financial costs, is painful to contemplate.

Volunteering at the dinner rekindled Paulie's relationships at Covenant House. From time to time, Deirdre, the executive director, texted or called him, inviting him to speak to the kids at the shelter about his life or grab a cup of coffee with her to catch up. She invited him to join her for the shelter's candlelight vigils, an annual outdoor event designed to remind people of the struggles of homeless teenagers as the winter closes in. Deirdre also invited Mildred, who had retired to Washington, D.C., asking both of them to stand with Covenant House supporters—elected officials, advocates, families, and friends—for the evening's program.

It was nine degrees as Paulie stood next to Mildred, both draped in down jackets, scarves, gloves, and hats. Deirdre took to the podium, her voice rising across West 6th Street to Town Square Park: "Every young person deserves a place to be warm and safe this winter. But more importantly, they deserve to know that they are special and beautiful and loved."

As the program ended and a children's choir finished singing, Paulie and Mildred locked arms and walked together from the stage into the warmth of Covenant House.

"You know, Paulie," Mildred said, as she smiled somewhat devilishly, "you are special and beautiful and loved."

"Yep," Paulie said with a grin. "So are you." A beat passed, but he could not help himself, "And trust me, Mildred, there were a lot of times I never thought I'd say that."

Homeless, but Graduating

Paulie's struggle to finish high school is typical of the challenges many homeless youth experience in school. Among the hundreds of young people who sought a bed at nine of the Covenant House shelters in North America in 2010, only 37 percent had a high school diploma or its equivalent. Without either, they often cannot find full-time employment and can quickly fall deeper into poverty and street life, especially in times of recession. All of Covenant House's U.S. shelters offer high school equivalency courses, and many innovative educational programs for homeless youth are worthy of replication. Education may very well be the single most important tool for young people aiming for self-sufficiency.

For example, advocates for homeless young people have championed a new cadre of schools, many of them created by charter, tailored to welcome homeless young people and meet their needs. The Center for Education Reform, a nonprofit group in Washington, D.C., that tracks charter schools, has contact with seven that specifically target homeless young people. In 2011, Broome Street Academy opened its doors to about 125 of New York City's most at-risk students, those who are homeless, in foster care, or come from very low-performing middle schools. The academy is on the third floor of The Door, a forty-year-old multiservice center for young people in Manhattan. Although The Door does not provide shelter, it offers almost everything else, including counseling, food, career services, health care, and legal aid, serving as a daytime refuge from the streets for many home-less youth. With a personalized program, the academy plans to tackle the issues that drive homeless and at-risk students away from school, while tripling the current graduation rates for this population.

Two charter school programs in the United States have taken the unusual step of operating through homeless shelters for youth: Covenant House Michigan in Detroit and the Academy of Urban Learning in Denver, Colorado. In 2005, Covenant House Michigan launched three charter high schools after Sam Joseph, the agency's founding executive director, estimated that 90 percent of the youth in the main shelter were high school dropouts. Although the charter school movement has been criticized for skimming the most motivated students and families away from the public school system, Covenant House Michigan actually helps the Detroit Public Schools by enrolling only dropouts and young people the system has expelled. On average, students at the schools are two to four years behind, and about 30 percent of them have been involved in the criminal justice system. A quarter are parents themselves.

Each school provides a team to work with students on their social and emotional needs, with counselors, a family liaison, and a psychologist. The schools try to move past whatever caused the young people to drop out in the first place—bullying, feeling in danger, hardships at home, not having clean clothes to wear.

More than 630 young people have earned their high school diplomas through Covenant House Michigan's schools in the last six years, although critics say the schools have four-year gradua-tion rates significantly lower than other Detroit charter schools, and test scores trail as well. That's understandable, given the hard-ships and the lack of support homeless young people face. School officials are working to show the value of schools that engage dis-connected and very transient homeless youth, breaking cycles of welfare dependency and incarceration that are not visible through the traditional school metrics.

Currently, almost 60 percent of the schools' graduates go on to some kind of formal, postsecondary training, either college, community college, trade schools, or certificate-granting programs. Covenant House Michigan's schools encourage graduates to push forward, knowing that a college degree more than doubles their likelihood of employment.

For the last twenty-five years, Youth on Their Own (YOTO), has helped homeless or abandoned young people ages thirteen to twenty-one graduate from high school in Tucson, Arizona. Supplying support services and a stipend of up to $125 a month to students who maintain good attendance and grades, the program has managed to shepherd 92 percent of its students to diplomas, in a state with only a 75 percent graduation rate.

In almost every high school in Tucson, the program works with school liaisons—school employees such as teachers, counselors, or dropout prevention specialists—who volunteer their time to Youth on Their Own as mentors, helping kids find clothing, health care, tutoring, job placements, college scholarships, and referrals to safe places to sleep. Community members have generously donated food items, clothing, bedding, diapers for the babies of young mothers, school supplies, household goods, and prom wear.

A little more than a third of YOTO's students are under the guardianship of the state of Arizona, because they have been abused or neglected by their parents; many live in group homes. The rest are eighteen- to twenty-one-year-olds who sleep from couch to couch, in subsidized apartments YOTO helps them find, or on the street. None of them go home to Mom and Dad at night, but they have a fierce desire to graduate.

The stipend, which is prorated according to what grades the kids earn, takes the edge off their poverty, said Teresa Liverzani-Baker, YOTO's executive director. For fifteen-year-olds whose parents have skipped out on them, leaving them with no money, no car, and no doctor, the stipend can help them avoid some crises.

The program to date has helped eighty-six hundred homeless young people in thirty schools and has given out thirty scholarships to a local two-year college, paid for by donors. The group was able to help about 570 of the 740 young people who applied in 2011, though Ms. Liverzani-Baker wishes they had reached more, to help each student, and to help Tucson as a whole. Homeless kids often stay in the city they grew up in, and if no one helps them become educated, they can grow into unemployable homeless adults.

She'd also like to expand the program around the country, but funding for a full-time staff person is needed to operate the program. It could be a dream job for the right person, to help young people graduate, even in the face of obstacles that they themselves had not created. A high school diploma, they know, is their ticket to get anywhere in life.

2

A Survivor Facing
Her Future
Muriel's Story

No one would sign up to be born with fetal alcohol syndrome, to be raised in a foreign culture, and to be depressed and addicted to drugs before turning thirteen. Yet this was Muriel's childhood. Before she was twenty, three different pimps had sold her body over the Internet countless times, for their own profit. Long before she broke free from the last one, someone at Covenant House said something that helped her find her footing: "You deserve better than this." The results prove what we tell people all of the time—our kids need to know that people believe in them. And when we convince them that they are amazing, just the way they are, they can reach the stars.

It was early in the morning, late in September 2010, a Monday, the day Sister Nancy Brown always heard appeals, one after another, from kids who wanted to come back to Covenant House Vancouver. They had all been discharged recently, for not following their plans, for fighting, or for being under the influence of drugs or alcohol. They all wanted a second chance, or a fifth. Or a sixth.

Sister Nancy, a gray-haired, neighborly woman with a hearty laugh, sat at a round table in her bright office, with a big quilt of the Tree of Life hanging on the wall. She looked across the table at Muriel, a nineteen-year-old with a vulnerable, shopworn beauty. The girl acted unhealthy and perplexed. Sister Nancy saw familiar signs of exhaustion and drugs but could also see the struggle in her—Muriel was working for an escort service, and part of her wanted to be safe instead. Sister Nancy, one of Vancouver's most visible opponents of sex trafficking, sensed a window of opportunity.

The staff had recently asked Muriel to leave because she was not following her plan, not trying hard enough to find a safe job. They worried that she was just refueling, enjoying a short respite before returning to work as an escort. From Sister Nancy's earlier work with domestic violence survivors, and now, after coming to understand the seedy underground of Vancouver, she knew the struggle to leave a dangerous situation needs to take priority over other goals. She knew the figures—between 85 and 95 percent of prostituted people want to leave their situations, but there are only a handful of shelter beds in North America available to them.

Although young people see Sister Nancy as an authority figure at first, she has a passion for justice, as well as a soft spot for earnest kids. Maybe, she thought, finding a job had not been the wisest priority for someone as young-looking as Muriel, who had a limited work history. When Muriel explained in a fast-flowing, girlish voice, "I'm really lost. I want to get my life back, get back into school, and do something, rather than traveling around with a suitcase," Sister Nancy knew what her answer to this appeal would be.

A member of the Sisters of Charity–Halifax who wears slacks and a sweater, rather than a habit, Sister Nancy felt grateful to work in a shelter where Muriel could be safe, where drugs and alcohol are not permitted, and where full-time addiction specialists are on staff. She vividly remembers the snapshots in the newspaper of the sad-eyed, disheveled victims of Willie Pickton, the pig farmer who confessed in 2007 to killing forty-nine women, mostly local prostituted and addicted people. His depravity still haunts the city.

Muriel appeared sincere and seemed less damaged by drugs than many of the sex trafficking victims Sister Nancy meets. Hardest to reach are the many girls who are doubly ensnared—by the threats and brainwashing that can come with prostitution, and by the physical and psychological ravages of addiction. Which problem do you tackle first? How do you help a young person realize that her pimp is manipulating her when he feeds her the drugs she craves? Would she go back to her pimp if kicking drugs proved too hard and she needed a free high? Would she go back to drugs to numb the pain of seeing with newly clear eyes how her pimp had exploited her or to avoid the pain of losing the relationship with him, which she had come to need?

Looking down at the five-foot-two, ninety-nine-pound woman-child across from her, Sister Nancy knew that any young person involved in prostitution was probably there because her family or community had rejected her. Sister Nancy had no interest in rejecting Muriel further and sending her back to the streets. There were already about ten thousand trafficked youth in Canada each year, and Sister Nancy wanted to help this girl step away from that life.

She said she was happy to see Muriel again and thanked her for returning. "I want you to come back into the shelter, rest, and start working on your plan," Sister Nancy said.

Muriel exhaled for what seemed like the first time all morning, as Sister Nancy encouraged her to think about her worth as a woman and as a person, so she could be strong in the choices she would make for herself. The nun asked her how the shelter could help her get her life back.

Muriel didn't know, exactly, but would try to figure it out during her fourth stay at the shelter. According to the antiseptic description in the daily Resident Logs, which includes counselor notes from each eight-hour shift, "youth indicated that she does not want to return to sex trade and really wants to return and live with her mother—must get job, work at schooling, stay clean and sober."

It was a formidable order. Sister Nancy would be watching, trying to help Muriel exit prostitution for good. As Muriel headed downstairs to rest, she shook her head at how much work it would take, just to get back home.

In the early 1990s in a tony suburb of Vancouver on the scenic west coast of Canada, a couple adopted a daughter from the Philippines. Three-year-old Muriel arrived in the family's neatly kept two-story home. It had a big picture window in front and a gracious cherry tree in the back. For a little girl born in a shack in Manila, the comfortable Canadian home, with a full pantry, looked like a wonderland.

Muriel's birth parents had been "engaged in different kinds of vices," according to her adoption records. She was the eighth of her birth mother's nine children and had lived with two different aunts before arriving in Canada, malnourished and suffering from intestinal parasites. She was a little beauty even then, pale, with big eyes and pouty lips, but she was also an impulsive and wild child, eating until she threw up, stealing things, and hoarding food, probably because she was not used to having a steady supply of it.

Muriel's adoptive mother had recently given birth to a third son, and three months after Muriel arrived, her adoptive father left the family. He visited on weekends, but the family mostly managed without him. Muriel knew him only as a part-time figure, one who, she felt, left the family because she had entered it. As she grew older, she wondered whether the others blamed her, seeing in her foreign face the cause of the family's dissolution.

Each time she looked in the mirror, she saw how different she was from them. Her brothers were brilliant and calm; she was energetic and manic. Her mother tried to channel her energy into ballet classes, but Muriel rarely sat still, setting fires, tampering with food, and playing around with her mother's medications. When pediatricians diagnosed her as having ADHD—attention deficit hyperactivity disorder—language processing difficulties, and oppositional defiant disorder, Muriel strung the labels next to all of the other words that defined her indelible differences from her family: adopted, foreign, hyper, girl. She could never shake the sense that she was not a part of their world.

Puberty hit Muriel with a vengeance. She was angry at being mismatched to her family and at her father's departure. At twelve, she started using drugs and became addicted to Ecstasy, which her friends supplied. Its chemical euphoria seemed to counteract the depression that gripped her. She spent hours biking around her neighborhood, which suited her perfectly, because she didn't want to go home. She ran away—a lot.

One day when she was fifteen, Muriel came home from school, then went upstairs to read for a couple of hours as usual. When she came downstairs, she saw her three brothers, her grandmother, her mother, and even her father, who rarely appeared on a weekday, all watching her. Something was clearly up. Why were they each standing in front of a doorway, barring any chance of escape?

Muriel recalled her family's steely demeanor as they told her they were sending her to the Philippines, that night, on a nine o'clock flight. She'd been out of control, she knew that. And now she was going to stay away until she learned how to be grateful. They had arranged for her to visit her birth family.

They were right to stand in front of the doors. She had no interest in visiting Manila. As a child, she had not been terribly curious about her birth family and had not fantasized about meeting them. From what she'd heard about her Filipino family, she was better off in Canada. She would not have been raised by her birth parents anyway. She knew her mother had more mouths to feed than she could handle and had planned to send infant Muriel to an orphanage instead.

So when she stepped off her flight alone in the Philippines the next day, there were no emotional embraces, only a taxi driver holding up a sign with her last name on it. She met her sisters, her brothers, an aunt, a nephew, a niece, her cousins, and finally her birth mother, who didn't speak English.

Muriel hated every single minute of the visit, every missed holiday back in Canada, and she grew more depressed. Each time she talked to her adoptive mother on the phone, she cried, begging to come home before Christmas. Her family in Canada promised to try to buy her a ticket by New Year's but didn't. When Muriel finally returned home after missing four and a half months of school, she felt deeply angry, and her resentment lasted for years.

Her parents soon realized that Manila had not been the panacea for Muriel that they needed. They offered to send Muriel to Outward Bound, a personal growth program set among the challenges of the wilderness, and to get her psychologically tested. They sent her to alternative schools and tried hard to find the proper medications for her behavioral problems, but nothing helped. She snuck out of the house at night and continued to do drugs. *Whatever*, Muriel thought. *Do whatever you guys think is going to make you feel better. It's truly going to make me want to do worse.*

She found one comfort at her mother's. A large cherry tree presiding over the backyard offered solace and steadiness as she watched it every day of the year, even though her mother wouldn't let her climb it. It bloomed, leafed out, turned dark red in autumn, fell barren, then budded out again. Its predictability calmed her. The tree's constancy gave her hope. It never died. It kept growing.

Muriel's mother worried that the same would not be true for her daughter. Just before Muriel's sixteenth birthday, her mother took her to the hospital, concerned that Muriel had a plan to kill herself—she still has light scars on her forearms where she cut herself. At the hospital, they asked her whether she wanted to go home. She didn't.

The day after her sixteenth birthday, Muriel entered foster care. From there, she spent two years drifting, from foster homes to friends' houses, back home for the night, holing up at safe houses (group shelters for homeless underage kids, where they can stay for a week at a time), trying a supervised apartment, all the while smoking a lot of pot, using a lot of Ecstasy and cocaine with friends, and skipping school.

Drugs were her only pleasure, and there wasn't a day between her seventeenth and eighteenth birthdays when she wasn't high. She believed she couldn't experience any natural happiness, and it made her so irritated that she kept cutting herself, which again landed her in the hospital when she was about eighteen.

A new personal low forced Muriel to realize that addiction had overtaken her. She had earned six hundred dollars for spending ten to fifteen minutes with a strange man with a foot fetish. She was high the whole time, but she later decided that the sexual experience was "gross." It was quick, easy cash that translated to as much cocaine as she wanted, but enough was enough. She went to her mother and asked for help.

Her mother set off in search of yet another possible solution, one Muriel finally seemed to want. The family found a rehab program in eastern British Columbia, where Muriel lasted almost six months before she was kicked out for fighting with another resident. If she had graduated, she could have returned home, her mother said, but now she had no other options. On May 6, 2010, she came back to Vancouver and made her way to Covenant House, which she had heard about while living at the safe houses.

She arrived dedicated to fighting her addictions. That first visit, she stayed a month and a half, until a fight with her mother sent Muriel off the deep end again, and she accepted a friend's invitation to go downtown to score some drugs. The friend, who was working in the escort business, introduced Muriel to her pimp, then went out for the night. At the end of a two-day binge, on top of the heroin, the Ecstasy, and the crack cocaine Muriel had already consumed, the pimp gave her GHB, a date-rape drug. It didn't make her pass out, though, because of all of the stimulants she had taken. He then spent hours trying to persuade her to work for him.

At the time, she was nineteen and had been a drug addict for seven years. Give her a drug, and she'd take it and keep on taking it, without stopping. The drugs won out, and she didn't fight back as the pimp, then his friend, had her. The pimp swiftly sent her to a hotel room and put her to work with a revolving door of strange johns.

She was young, Asian, and lovely. There was no shortage of demand for her. She describes the johns disdainfully, how full of themselves they sounded, their tendency to show off their houses and brag about their careers. There was an old man who lived by the yacht club downtown, a milkman who just wanted to talk, a guy or two who had just gotten out of jail, married men who would pay six hundred dollars an hour. There was a steady stream of them during the total of four months she worked as an escort for three different pimps—at least two calls a day, sometimes eight or nine. They were mostly boastful, self-involved men, and they used her body, sometimes roughly, never tenderly. She was not fully a person to them; the encounters hinged on their fantasies. This was not about intimacy, love, or connection. The pimps made sure that the drugs kept her numb.

Homeless young people such as those who come to Covenant House are those most likely to be ensnared by sex traffickers, who do not exploit only young people from abroad: 83 percent of confirmed sex-trafficking incidents in the United States involved U.S. citizens as victims, according to the federally funded anti–human trafficking task forces within the United States.

Kids with no place to stay often come to the attention of pimps, who troll the streets around youth homeless shelters, hang out in nearby pizza parlors and schools, patrol bus terminals and airports, and even send young recruiters to live inside shelters to lure young people into the sex trade. They quickly find the kids who have no strong father figures in their lives, a history of foster care or sexual abuse, broken family bonds, or problems with addiction. Kids without belief in themselves or hope for their futures are vulnerable to anyone offering so much as a free lunch.

These aren't the kids who can easily say no to a sweet-talking grownup who tells them they're gorgeous and takes them shopping for name-brand clothes, pretending to be a boyfriend who cares about them. Many young female victims of the sex trade—and victims are predominantly female—become brainwashed and isolated, believing they are in love with their pimps, holding out hope that the only close relationship they know could somehow turn healthy.

Accurate figures for victims of human trafficking in the United States and Canada are hard to come by, and for good reason— pimps often hide their workers away from the public eye and train them not to give their real names or ages if they are arrested. Moreover, prostituted young people don't often seek help from the authorities, who are at least as likely to arrest them as to help them. Many don't see themselves as trafficking victims at all, but they are, under U.S. and Canadian law, both of which define child trafficking as forcing anyone under eighteen to engage in a commercial sex act. For people over eighteen to be considered trafficking victims in the United States, they must have been made to engage in a commercial sex act through "force, fraud, coercion" or any combination of the three. To be considered a trafficking victim under Canadian law, one must fear for one's safety or the safety of someone known to them, a higher standard that makes enforcement more difficult, a rule Sister Nancy and other advocates are working to eliminate.

The number of U.S. youth at risk of being trafficked ranges from 100,000 to 300,000, according to a University of Pennsylvania study—a number that some critics have claimed is too high. The

Justice Department estimates that of the nation's 1.6 million run-away or throwaway young people each year, 38,600 were at risk of sexual endangerment or exploitation as of 1999, while UNICEF estimates that 1.2 million children worldwide are victims of commercial sexual exploitation each year.

Between 2001 and 2008, the U.S. Department of Juvenile Justice and Delinquency Prevention tallied twelve thousand two hundred arrests of minors for prostitution or "commercialized vice," and the number caught is certainly far lower than the number involved in such offenses. The Federal Bureau of Investigation's forty-six Innocence Lost task forces and working groups have recovered or identified more than two thousand trafficking victims, secured 927 convictions of those who exploit children, and seized more than $3.1 million in assets since 2003. Between January 2008 and June 2010, state and local police departments involved in human trafficking task forces conducted 1,016 investigations of sex trafficking where the alleged victims were under eighteen.

The scope of the human trafficking epidemic can also be seen city by city. In 2006, the Center for Court Innovation found 3,946 commercially sexually exploited children in New York City. One police sergeant there estimated that each year, 3,000 runaways or young people in danger of being exploited go through the Port Authority Bus Terminal alone, near Covenant House's oldest and largest shelter.

In 2010, Seattle police found eighty-one prostituted young people, more than double the number found in 2009. In Winnipeg, Manitoba, about four hundred children and young people are believed to be trafficked annually, and that's only counting those who work on the street. More than three-quarters of those kids had previously lived under the supervision of Manitoba's Child and Family Services.

Meanwhile, the pimps operate with impunity, realizing that law enforcement has not considered them a priority: the U.S.

government battles human trafficking with only 0.1 percent of what it spends on fighting the drug trade. Many criminal gangs have noticed and have traded in drug sales for the more profitable and low-risk sale of people, in part because women and girls, unlike drugs, can be sold over and over again for someone else's profit. In addition, those girls seldom seek help from police. Some are more apt to bail out their victimizers than to turn them in.

One Canadian study shows that prostituted women and girls face a mortality rate 40 times higher than average women do. Even if they are able to leave and steer clear of a pimp's influence and attempts to lure them back, there are limited resources to address their overwhelming range of needs. Many need to visit doctors and obtain medication. Many young trafficking victims, such as Muriel, never had the chance to finish school or develop any job skills at all, and their relationships with their families are flimsy at best, so they often lack a trusted adult to help them through this most difficult transition. Many, such as Muriel, need intensive help in overcoming addictions, and most need long-term psychological counseling—in one study, 68 percent of prostituted people suffered from post-traumatic stress syndrome.

Arriving at Covenant House

After three months of working as an escort, Muriel left her pimp and tried to recover her earnings from him. He stole her dog, a long-haired Chihuahua, and put his foot on its neck, threatening to kill it in front of her if she didn't stay with him. She refused. She figured that in the three months she had been working for him, she had probably made eighty thousand dollars and was supposed to have half of it. He refused. (She later learned that the dog had survived.)

She returned to the safety of Covenant House, but she was still using drugs and was unwilling to address her addiction. Resistant to job hunting, Muriel idled away the weeks until the staff asked her to make a decision: begin seriously looking for work or make alternative living arrangements. She bolted but a few days later found herself pleading with Sister Nancy for a third chance, which was granted. Muriel came back to Covenant House, where she was glad to see Crystal Schwarz, twenty-five, a youth worker Muriel had known from an earlier safe house. Muriel liked that Crystal, who has long brown hair and a pleasant, round face, was close to her age and cheerful.

One night after the regular residents' meeting, on the first floor of the Drake Street shelter, Muriel was hanging out in the big beige common room near the television and the coffee table. She sat in one of the black swivel chairs, hitting it with the drumsticks from the Wii's Rock Band game.

"Muriel, do you need to talk? I think you need to talk," Crystal said. Muriel didn't think so, but she managed to chat about how she liked a certain boy. As the conversation progressed, past more gossip and "I hate it when parents do that, don't you?" Muriel began unloading what she was feeling at the moment and, eventually, about how upset she was after hearing that her former pimp had stabbed a girl in the throat. She admitted that she'd felt more depressed during the last few months, frustrated with her addiction and her need for the money she made at glamorous parties where her pimp made her work. She burst into tears, something she had almost never done at home. What had been the point, there? She felt as if no one had listened to her, and it had become easier to detach from her pain by abusing drugs, to stop feeling and thinking.

Now, Crystal jumped in to offer comfort. "You're a valuable person, and you have a lot of reasons to feel good about yourself," she told Muriel. "Look at how strong you've had to be to get this far. You deserve better than this." The conversations with Crystal, soon a nightly habit, were hard but necessary. As the weeks passed, Muriel came to cherish Crystal's ability to listen and her refreshing willingness to take Muriel seriously. "I think I just never had someone I could sit down and talk with and be able to free the dam of tears," Muriel explained.

The Covenant House counselors noted in the log one weekday in the fall of 2010 that it was going to be a "heavy" day for Muriel. The results were due from her psychological tests at a local children's diagnostic center, and the staff suspected they would be hard to hear.

A few months earlier, she had been completely annoyed to have to attend a daylong evaluation of her mental functioning, at her mother's insistence. She had still been working for an escort service and using drugs at the time, and she was the oldest patient at the center by about twelve years. She felt that everyone talked to her with a "goo goo gah gah" tone of voice, and she hated being at the center a full nine hours, being asked about squiggly lines and the meanings of blotches. Beyond all of that, she had never done particularly well on tests, and the long day of testing made her head spin.

The results of the tests showed her to have been affected by exposure to alcohol before she was born. She had "alcohol-related neurodevelopmental disorder," a form of fetal alcohol syndrome. The disorder's symptoms sounded familiar—sleep disturbances, attention and learning deficits, and difficulties with emotional bonds. Her test scores showed serious problems with following rules, keeping safe, and regulating her behavior.

Fetal alcohol spectrum disorders (FASD), a range of disorders that includes fetal alcohol syndrome, may well be one of the most daunting diagnoses a young person can receive. The painful consequences are all the more maddening because they stem from someone else's actions. According to Muriel's diagnostic report, people with the disorder have difficulty keeping consequences in mind while making decisions, which leads to a pattern of making choices that aren't in their best interests. Many people with the disorder can be easily manipulated and often act out sexually, a combination ripe for exploitation.

One study from the U.S. Centers for Disease Control and Prevention showed that more than half of adolescents with the condition had been suspended from school, almost 30 percent had been expelled, and a quarter had dropped out. About 60 percent of adolescents and adults with FASD have been in trouble with the law, and about half of adolescents show inappropriate sexual behaviors. Many have difficulty forming emotional attachments, which may explain the numerous challenging issues Muriel faced in childhood but which also saved her from falling in love with her pimps. The syndrome is basically a prediction of likely lifelong failure—80 percent of people with it can't live independently, and almost half of all adults with the syndrome have alcohol and drug problems. Young people do much better if the condition is discovered before they are six. Muriel was nineteen.

Muriel was hanging out with the staff members in one of their offices when she first read the report of her test results. "Stupid people, who do they think they are?" she railed, not recognizing the girl described in the report. Crystal just listened, heavy-hearted that Muriel was taking the news so hard but hoping that it would help her in the end—that an understanding of her diagnosis would make it more possible for her to overcome her problems. Although the diagnosis provided an explanation for a number of puzzling behaviors during her young life, Muriel looked at it more as a downright insult. She did not want to feel broken, and it galled her that the news essentially bolstered what she saw as her mother's belief that Muriel could never meet the family's goals for her.

For months at the shelter, Muriel had struggled to earn her way back to her mother's home. The staff noticed how Muriel's mother seemed uncomfortable with the idea, perhaps worn down by years of rebellion, domestic strife, and searches for fruitless yet expensive solutions. She erected hurdles for Muriel to cross, with the promise of welcoming her home, but then reneged and established new obstacles. It happened time and again: Muriel could come home if she returned to school, then if she quit drugs, but the goal post receded every time Muriel made progress.

The phenomenon is not uncommon among parents who have struggled with their children's behavior for years and then relish the peace at home once their son or daughter is gone. Many parents worry that they are unprepared to manage their children's behavior on their return, and without appropriate support services, they may be right.

Gradually, with the help of regular therapy at the shelter, Muriel realized that she was never going to meet her mother's ever-changing expectations and had to live for herself. It would take time.

Muriel's friend beamed with pride as she showed Muriel her pimp's apartment in Gastown, the hip neighborhood known for its gaslights and cobblestone streets that bordered Vancouver's harbor. The two-bedroom apartment had a stainless steel kitchen, a beautiful balcony, and access to a sauna, a pool, and a fitness room. It looked like an elegant set-up, half a world away from Muriel's shared room in the shelter. In fact, it was a "micro-brothel," accommodating one or two prostituted girls, easily hidden from the police, often found nowadays in high-rise condominiums and upper-income neighborhoods.

The girlfriend called Muriel a few nights later, asking her to come live there. Muriel quickly told her counselors she was going back to turning tricks. She had grieved over her time in prostitution, but she could not shake its pull. Sister Nancy recognized the pattern, having seen a number of trafficking victims go back to prostitution while in the process of breaking free of it. And Muriel was free to leave—Covenant House's central principles include the belief that young people choose their own paths, even if that means going backward sometimes. Transformation does not hold up any other way.

Yet when Muriel left, she took with her a certain phrase that hounded her. Somebody at Covenant House, no one remembers who, had planted a stubborn seed within her.

"They told me, 'It's your decision to go back,'" Muriel said, "and also, 'You're so much better than that.'"

Crystal felt deeply sad to see her go but remembered how Muriel had struggled with prostitution's strong grip, often confessing that she didn't know whether she could give up the drugs and the money. Of course, Muriel didn't ever have control over her income. She learned that early on when her first pimp took her shopping for fancy clothes, bought with money she had already earned for him by having loveless sex with a parade of johns.

When she was "working," the PI's, as she called her three successive pimps, dominated her life, never leaving her alone, hacking into her phone, keeping her on a strict diet, making her and the other girls wake up at six o'clock, and working them almost all of the time. Her pimps kept drugging her with GHB, the date rape drug or "G," which, when mixed with alcohol, makes people black out. It is often a sexual stimulant, and the pimps tricked her into taking it by mixing it with the cocaine she craved. The combination compelled her to do what she didn't want to do.

She found herself struggling with her own addictions and adding a new one—energy drinks. Her pimp forbade her to sleep until she had turned a trick, so she filled a wall of her apartment with the empties of Red Bulls and Monsters. "I was in pretty deep," Muriel said.

Lisa Ronaldson, a Covenant House Vancouver case manager, remembers working the overnight shift and watching the shameless behavior of the pimps affiliated with a local motorcycle gang. "They would bring us in people, and say, 'Could you clean up these people? They're not making a profit for me.'" The pimps tried to use Covenant House as a way to heal their "investments," bringing girls and young women in when they were menstruating, to let them sleep for a week. During those stays, counselors tried to show the prostituted young women that their pimps and the whole system considered them easily dispensable. Sometimes it worked, sometimes not.

HELPING TRAFFICKING VICTIMS, HOLDING EXPLOITERS ACCOUNTABLE

Advocates have discovered many new weapons against the commercial sexual exploitation of young people, but these need to be deployed more widely. In 1999, for example, Sweden passed a law against the purchasing of sex, considering it a violation of human rights and women's rights. The law criminalizes the client and the pimp, while asserting that prostituted people are most often victims of coercion and trafficking and should not be punished.

The Swedish legal system actively prosecutes and punishes johns; offenders can face fines based on their income, and a john can go to jail if the purchase of sex is made through organized prostitution. It seems to be working. In the law's first year, arrests increased 300 percent. Now, fewer johns are trying to buy sex, the number of women working on the streets has decreased between 30 and 50 percent, recruitment has nearly stopped, and the estimated number of women in prostitution dropped from twenty-five hundred to fifteen hundred in three years. Traffickers are looking elsewhere to set up shop.

Yet that's Sweden (and Norway, Iceland, the Philippines, and South Korea, which adopted similar measures, now known as the Nordic Model). North America has been slower to understand that children who sell their bodies for the financial gain of others and anyone forced into prostitution are trafficking victims. In the United States, police too often arrest a prostituted person without assessing whether she or he is being coerced or is in physical danger.

Demand for sexually exploited young people can be reduced simply by enforcing existing laws. Police need to become more aggressive with sting operations to find pimps and johns. Police academies need to train officers to look for the signs of trafficking, much as they strengthened their instruction on domestic violence intervention in the wake of new reform laws decades ago. As more prostitution businesses move inside, through Internet advertising and the use of micro-brothels, police can partner with building and restaurant inspectors, who often run across hidden trafficked people.

Advocates for victims have suggestions for making the penalties for buying sex commensurate with the crime. In Chicago, for example, the police now post on their website pictures of those who have been arrested for solicitation or related crimes. Norma Ramos, the executive director of the Coalition Against the Trafficking of Women, advocates impounding johns' vehicles—most of the men are married and would find it hard to explain where they left the minivan. She also recommends putting any man who buys sex on the sex offender list.

It's important to tackle the supply side, too, said Rachel Lloyd, the executive director and founder of Girls Educational & Mentoring Services (GEMS), a nonprofit group based in New York City that serves trafficked girls and young women. "We have to address poverty, race, class, child abuse, domestic violence, things people don't really want to talk about regarding this issue," she said. More homeless teenagers mean more potential trafficking victims.

Indeed, kids who are trafficked often lack a parent or a mentor to watch out for them. Keeping kids connected to their families, trusted relatives, and other adults and their communities can protect them from exploitation on the streets.

In the end, Muriel got scared straight—she saw a friend descend into addiction to Oxycontin and started seeing people she thought were her friends turn more distrustful the longer they worked. She kept wondering whether this was what she wanted to do for the rest of her life, and she began to see more of the dangers of prostitution. Although she had felt invincible at the beginning, that feeling was long gone. When one of the johns pushed a girl down a flight of thirty-five stairs in a rage, Muriel suddenly felt in danger.

"That could've been one of our calls," she said. "You can be that girl on the news, that Jane Doe wherever they put the bodies. Everyone's so much better than that."

That phrase kept coming back to her, as she tried to make the break with her addictions and the wild parties. She realized that she no longer wanted to be that prostitute, that junkie. She wasn't happy anymore, in her ongoing retreat from reality. It was time to go back to Covenant House. During the last year, she had left prostitution twice, only to return again. But this time, she resolved to break free for good.

.   .   .

When Muriel returned to the shelter for the fifth and final time in December 2010, that voice saying "you are better" had become her own. She reunited with Crystal, who helped her with a peculiar rite of passage—together, they gently pried off her fake nails. Muriel celebrated the rejecting of that tell-tale glamour and started working hard to quit drugs.

Still, in late October 2010, Muriel worried that prostitution might not be done with her. Her Resident Log reads, "10/27: youth redisciosed her run-in with her old pimp who threatened her life when she left. Youth is feeling unsafe to leave shelter alone, thus is allowed to stay in through the week, over the weekend and until she feels safe. Crime Stoppers was called and file is open." Muriel pressed charges against the pimp, who was allegedly wanted for attempted murder at the time.

The Muriel who first came to Covenant House would not have taken such a courageous step. With the help of weekly group therapy and speaking regularly to a psychiatrist, to Crystal, and to her other counselors, Muriel had learned how to make better decisions and become more confident, Sister Nancy said. Her choices also became wiser as she began her recovery from addiction. Whenever Muriel spoke with Sister Nancy, she hoped she could prove she was making good decisions. "Whenever I look into her eyes, it's like she's not just looking at me, but imagining me, what I can do," Muriel said. Sister Nancy's belief in Muriel helped keep Covenant House's doors open for her, over and over, until she was able to break away from the pimps, drug dealers, johns, and traffickers who had taken control of her days and nights.

Muriel wanted to tell her story specifically to encourage young people who are still being trafficked. She wants them to know that if she escaped, others can as well. She shakes her head, because what she is about to say sounds hard to believe: "We're the ones with the power. With power you can make it stop."

Now, she never considers returning to prostitution. A young woman she knew from that period had called her about three months earlier and asked whether she ever thought about working again. She looked at the phone incredulously. "What, and lose your dignity all over again? That's the way it is for some girls. It's something they think they can go back to whenever they please. I'm an adult now. I really need to get my life back on track."

As her last stay at Covenant House drew to a close, Muriel no longer fidgeted when she talked to her counselors and had regained the physical confidence of a dancer, the young ballerina reemerging. She had enjoyed recent hip-hop classes near the shelter and wanted to start them up again after she found a place of her own. Her body was hers once more.

In April 2011, Muriel moved into a bright, furnished one-bedroom apartment with a view of Vancouver's North Shore mountains. She qualified for affordable housing through Community Living British Columbia (CLBC), a provincial government organization that helps people living with disabilities, providing landlords who are trained and paid to give supportive services. Muriel is attending adult school classes, aiming to earn her high school diploma, and charting a course through college, to study social work, to be a counselor.

She likes Vancouver and its hills, in contrast to the flatness of the suburbs. She likes her new apartment and feels hopeful now. The highlights of her new life pounce and tumble around the floor and jump up among the dinner plates. Muriel is taking care of three black cats, though that grew to nine for a bit, recently. One, Lovey, is hers; the other two, Moose and Addie, belong to the young woman who lives next door. Muriel is watching the cats while her neighbor is away.

The cats get Muriel through her days. She cuddles them and pets them and feeds them treats mixed with catnip. When Moose was a day away from giving birth, Muriel could barely leave the house or stop checking for signs of imminent kittens.

The apartment is neat, sparsely furnished, with plenty of room for her to dance in her bedroom by herself. She is *home*, and the word has a new meaning for her. "Now I would say home would be somewhere where my cats are, where I'm happy—comfortable, safe, and meaningful. I do not want to have kids for a long time, but these little babies give me something to wake up to and care for, other than myself. I'd rather spend time on something or somebody else, like these little buggers."

She calls Covenant House her escape ticket, and she wants to work there as a counselor one day and help other trafficking survivors. Crystal predicts Muriel could be very successful in the job, because she had been so supportive of other residents, helping them through the recent death of a young man who previously stayed at the shelter and encouraging her peers to go to dance classes or Narcotics Anonymous meetings with her. She could make a very credible advocate about issues facing homeless young people, and has already spoken at a recent local summit about homelessness.

Like the cherry tree in her mother's yard, the one that comforted her through a bleak adolescence, Muriel is preparing to bloom, at last.

Fighting Back on Many Fronts

Muriel has a list of suggestions for helping young people escape from prostitution: lock away pimps and criminalize massage parlors, for starters. In addition, more people need to hear the truth about the deceits of traffickers who exploit runaways and other young people at risk.

In the United States adopting the Nordic Model—aggressively punishing people who buy sex, rather than only those who sell it—would go far in reducing the demand for prostitutes. In many jurisdictions, the laws are there, ready to be enforced. All it would take is the political will, which advocates can help sway.

In Canada, where prostitution is legal in some circumstances, but operating a brothel, procuring, and soliciting for sex in public are illegal, advocates are already urging the government to adapt the Nordic Model by toughening its laws against traffickers and increasing its enforcement efforts. Even though Canada has adopted trafficking prohibitions into its Criminal Code, their tighter definition of trafficking stymies many investigations and makes convictions more difficult, according to Sister Nancy.

Although advocates of legalizing prostitution promise greater regulation of the sex industry and safer conditions for those working in it, such visions have not come true. After countries such as New Zealand, Australia, and the Netherlands legalized or decriminalized prostitution, they saw an increase in human trafficking, in illegal brothels, and in organized crime. In fact, the mayor of Amsterdam called the experiment with legalization "an abysmal failure." Sister Nancy agrees, saying, "Any time prostitution has been legalized, there is an expansion of the industry, an increase of human trafficking, and the normalizing of sexual exploitation."

Underage prostitution has been called the only form of child abuse where the child, not the abuser, is routinely put behind bars. As of 2012, seven U.S. states have passed Safe Harbor for Sexually Exploited Youth Acts, which treat minors arrested for prostitution as victims. Trafficked children then receive shelter and services, instead of a sentence to juvenile detention. More states need to pass Safe Harbor Acts and consider extending protections for trafficking victims up to age twenty-one. Child prostitution is often statutory rape, because many victims sent out to sell their bodies for the profit of others are too young to give legal consent. And what about the eighteen- to twenty-one-year-old trafficking victims at Covenant House who are too old for safe harbor laws? Statistically, these young people were most likely forced into prostitution as children or adolescents, but any previous attempts at escape likely led not to freedom, but to beatings by a trafficker. They also need justice.

Traffickers have recently found very easy ways to advertise young people for sale—adult Internet sites provide anonymous access to countless customers—but public officials are fighting back. State attorneys general succeeded in 2010 in pressuring Craigslist.com to shut down its erotic advertising section, and they have called for Backpage.com to follow suit. The website, owned by Village Voice Media Holdings, is expected to earn $24.8 million annually from "adult" ads, accounting for two-thirds of that market. Some city officials have taken prominent stands against human trafficking, including Seattle mayor Mike McGinn, who called out Backpage.com for its erotic ads. Village Voice Media Holdings also owns the *Seattle Weekly*, and the mayor smartly ordered the city to withhold all of its advertising from the paper until Village Voice Media strengthens its procedures against running child prostitution ads, by requiring people in erotic ads to present photo identification in person, so that their ages could be verified.

That idea has already spread statewide. A law passed in Washington State in early 2012 makes it a felony to advertise the sexual services of juveniles. The law requires print and online publishers, including Backpage.com, to verify that a person whose services are advertised is over eighteen, as confirmed by legal documents such as birth certificates or driver's licenses.

Anti-trafficking activists, nonprofit groups, and law enforcement officials have worked together to fight the sexual exploitation of children on a local level. Members of the Philadelphia Anti-Trafficking Coalition scan the back pages of the *Philadelphia Weekly* and the *City Paper* for ads for massage parlors and adult services, looking for warning signs that the businesses may be using forced labor. A red flag goes up if an ad says "in call" (which means clients have to go to the business and the business's workers are not allowed to come to them) or talks about young women of particular ethnicities. Hugh Organ, the associate executive director of Philadelphia's Covenant House and the head of the coalition, works with outreach workers to stake out such businesses, which are usually located in unmarked buildings in rundown neighborhoods with the windows covered so no one can see inside. The typical business looks dilapidated but has new video cameras in the front. Mr. Organ and his coworkers talk to neighbors to see whether they have observed suspicious activities, and they distribute literature to neighbors and possible sex anti-trafficking victims, in a way that won't get the young women in trouble with their pimps. The anti-trafficking campaign can notify the police or the FBI about suspicious sites. It distributes the federal hotline number for victims who need help and is pushing a law to require all hotels, motels, truck stops, and bars to post the number. The hotline, 1-888-373-7888, is run by the National Human Trafficking Resource Center, a program of the Polaris Project, a nonprofit, nongovernmental organization fighting human trafficking.

Since the middle of 2011, Covenant House International has run the Abolish Child Trafficking website (AbolishChildTrafficking.org), which provides action alerts, shares survivors' stories and statistics about the sexual exploitation of children, and compiles actions that people have taken to fight trafficking, such as lobbying for important national and local legislation.

Of course, once they break free, trafficking victims require safe escape routes, including an education, job training, and counseling. "We need to offer them opportunities and choices, because they're not going to go work for eight dollars an hour when they can make five hundred dollars a night," said Lisa Ronaldson of Covenant House Vancouver.

Girls Educational & Mentoring Services (GEMS), a nonprofit group based in New York City, reports a 72 percent success rate in helping girls escape the commercial sex industry, according to Rachel Lloyd, its founder. Other groups, including Genesis House in Vancouver, British Columbia; Breaking Free in St. Paul, Minnesota; Dignity in Phoenix, Arizona; Children of the Night in Van Nuys, California; FAIR Girls in Washington, D.C.; and Veronica's Voice in Kansas City, Kansas, provide housing and/or comprehensive services to people trying to escape prostitution. Financial assets seized from convicted pimps and johns need to be directed to safe shelters, where recovering survivors can receive services while separated from the influence of their exploiters.

Ms. Lloyd, one of the country's most influential anti-trafficking advocates, feels optimistic that the problem of sex trafficking can be tackled as more people become informed about it. Young people need to know the dangers of sexual exploitation and of traffickers' tricks for luring new victims. Canada's "Kids in the Know" program, with lessons for every grade level, covers personal safety and the prevention of child sexual exploitation (KidsInTheKnow.ca/). FAIR Girls provides a series of workshops called "Tell Your Friends" to local public high schools, to help teens talk about healthy and unhealthy dating relationships, commercial sexual exploitation, and human trafficking, and in Boston, similar "My Life, My Choice" trainings have been held in group homes, child protective services offices, juvenile justice facilities, and schools. GEMS does trainings in the New York City public schools, and Ms. Lloyd stresses the importance of training adults as well as students, so that kids with concerns can find knowledgeable and sympathetic advisers.

Work is needed on a more broad level as well, she said. "We have to change how boys and young men are socialized around this issue, believing that it's okay to grow up to buy women and girls. We're raising boys in a culture that's continuously saying this is all right, normal, something that makes you a man." Such messages must be delivered, at home and at school, sooner rather than later.

3

Moving Forward after Foster Care
Benjamin's Story

Benjamin was the first young person interviewed for this book, and it was inspiring to shadow him as he walked the halls of a junior high school in a rough neighborhood, helping at-risk students make it through the first years of adolescence. Here was someone paying it forward, passing along the respect and love he had first found not at home, but at Covenant House, then on the football field, and ultimately with the circle he now calls family. The more we learned of his story, especially from reading thousands of pages in his Child Protective Services file, the more we felt in awe of his journey.

Benjamin Baker stepped off the bus from college, living life in reverse. About a week earlier he had arrived at Cisco Junior College, ready to play football, in the best shape of his life. The campus rose up from farm-to-market roads and fields planted in bluebonnet flowers, about as far from the ghetto of his childhood as he could get and still be in Texas. Yet during one of the grueling, "two-a-day" practices before school officially starts, he clowned around, trying to make others laugh. An assistant coach became angry and punished him with a particularly hard extra workout in the midday August sun. The pain, the taunts, the humiliation— they were too close to Benjamin's secret childhood traumas, and his rage bubbled over. The head coach kicked him out, and a sheriff's officer escorted him to a bus back to Houston.

As Benjamin settled down under the overpass of the Gulf Freeway, across from the Greyhound station, it hit him. No system was in charge of him anymore. Life was real. He'd had a full scholarship to play ball, and he messed it up, being a hard-headed twenty-year-old. At six foot six, with a magnetic grin and Clark Kent glasses complementing his Superman jawline, he could have been a big man on campus. Now, with no plan, he walked the streets during the day and fell asleep under the bridge at night, laying his head on a pile of trash bags balled together for a pillow, sometimes waking up with his face in the dirt. He tried to keep in shape, doing push-ups and sit-ups on patches of grass littered with broken glass.

His family refused to take him in, and he was too embarrassed to reach out to the people who had helped him earn a spot at Cisco. He was a living, breathing statistic, one of the nearly 40 percent of young people who age out of foster care at eighteen and become homeless before their midtwenties. With his stomach noisy and sore from hunger, Benjamin even started to miss foster care. Texas Child Protective Services might have been unforgivably erratic in sending him to dozens of different placements in eleven years, but at least it had put a roof over his head and food in his belly.

He started working with a drug dealer, helping to collect debts. Once in a while, he walked onto the campus of the University of Houston, which he had wanted to attend as a child. Wearing clothes from a thrift store, he listened to people talk as they headed to business or law classes. The students sounded intellectual and well spoken. Once again he felt like an outsider, once again that kindergartener with scarred hands and pee-stained pants whom no one liked. Maybe his expulsion from Cisco was the right move, even if it had not been his decision. College was not for him, no way. He'd go back to the bridge and think.

As he tells his story today, it is hard to imagine Benjamin as a small, vulnerable child. At twenty-nine, he weighs 255 pounds and shaves his head every two days. His handshake is powerful—he has bench-pressed 495 pounds—but the dark brown skin of his hands is tight and speckled with variegated scars from numerous grafts, the only physical evidence of a miserable childhood.

Benjamin Baker was born in Houston, Texas, in the summer of 1982, the third of five children. When he was eighteen months old, his mother, Camille, scalded his hands with hot water, and he suffered third-degree burns. Benjamin was rushed to the hospital, and the police arrested Camille, who went to jail for four months. His father, Claude, disappeared from the official radar screen for several years.

Benjamin, his brother, and one sister fell into the custody of Texas Child Protective Services (CPS), which took them to live with their grandmother. His siblings stayed for a short while before returning home, but Benjamin stayed on with his mother's mother. She loved him dearly, and he loved her right back. She went to church four times a week and was the best cook ever, famous for her hot-water corn bread and her snap beans. She called out the Bakers for being harsh with the children and encouraged Camille to divorce Claude, whom she blamed for Camille's deteriorating mental health. She protected Benjamin. As if she needed a reminder of the importance of her task, she began her days by seeing Benjamin's slowly healing hands reach out to her for a hug.

Yet as much as he loved his grandma, Benjamin longed to be reunited with his family, who lived on the other side of a four-lane road in one of the roughest parts of Houston. He had no memory of his mother burning his hands, but he'd heard caseworkers and relatives talk about it. Benjamin repeatedly hatched escape plans to visit his mother and siblings. Not yet old enough for kindergarten, he snuck out of his grandmother's house, down the street, and to the edge of the busy road with no median strip, hoping to reach his home.

Before he ever made it across, his grandmother, alerted by the neighbors, swept down and hustled him back home. She knew this was one of the most gang-infested areas in the city, and she wasn't about to let her grandson walk into busy traffic, an open-air drug market, or her daughter's troubled home.

At age five, while visiting with his parents in court, Benjamin asked his mother why she had burned his hands. She told him she had been hearing voices, but he didn't understand. When he was six, in part because of his wishes, CPS sent him back to live with the Bakers, because his mother had finished up her probation and had attended counseling and parenting classes. Resentful of Camille's mother's influence over his family, Claude forbade her to visit the children. Benjamin doesn't remember ever seeing his grandmother again.

He could have used her help. As discipline, Benjamin's parents often ordered him to stand in a corner naked for up to sixteen hours at time. His siblings kept watch, letting him know when the grownups stepped away, telling him when he could sit down. He worked hard to stay on his siblings' good side: he needed them to make it through life in the apartment.

Benjamin wet his bed frequently. He tried not to, but he was afraid to use the toilet at night, because his father would sometimes hide in the shower or behind the bathroom door, then jump out at him. His parents made him copy "I will not wet the bed" thousands of times. They put him to bed in his school clothes, and when he awoke wet, they shamed him in front of the neighbors, leaning his mattress outside with a chalkboard next to it that read,

"This is Benjamin's pissy bed." They ironed his wet clothes to dry them, and they sent him to school the next day in the same reeking outfit. As if the nights weren't dark enough, Benjamin remembers his father routinely molesting him.

Benjamin could hear the other children in the classroom laughing loudly behind him, mocking his scars and his stench, taunting him. He shoved his hands in his pockets. Sitting at his desk, Benjamin could hear snickers all around him—"Hey, Mr. Pee-body," "Hey, pissy."

The neighborhood offered no comfort. His apartment complex of two-story brick barracks on starkly flat land was so crime-ridden that the police set up an outpost right across the street. He saw a man get stabbed with a machete, one get beaten with a pool stick, and another attacked with a lock used as brass knuckles. Whenever he heard gunfire, he hit the dirt.

When social workers from CPS visited the home, they asked the children whether they were being abused. All of them denied it, including Benjamin, afraid of the repercussions. CPS didn't see anything unusual going on, and Benjamin did not tell them about the molestation, which lasted until he was nine. Afraid his family would hurt him more, he kept quiet. In the three years he lived at home, between the ages of six and nine, he was admitted to psychiatric hospitals three times for threatening to kill himself.

When Benjamin was nine, Camille came to school with a belt, threatening to beat him for mistakes on his homework. She was mad at what she considered his messy penmanship, even though he was earning As in handwriting. Camille said that a teacher's aide had called her to say he was acting up, but no aide had called. The school official who reported her to child welfare said that Benjamin had old and recent marks and scabs on his body from being hit with a belt, and he was afraid to go home: "He said he doesn't like his mother, because she messed up his hands. He said he wants to have hands like everybody else. He said he wants new hands."

His family's dysfunctions are painted clearly in Benjamin's thirty-one-hundred-page case record from the Texas child welfare agency. The investigation of the school's concerns noted that Camille admitted whipping him with a belt every time he misbehaved. Benjamin said he was beaten daily. Camille agreed not to use physical discipline on Benjamin anymore, but her promise was meaningless.

The case was closed, Benjamin was sent back home, and a social worker was assigned to monitor the family once a month. Texas child welfare officials did not remove Benjamin from his mother's home for another seven and a half months, which in the Baker household likely meant two hundred more beatings.

MEMORIES OF MISTREATMENT

Benjamin enjoyed school, even though the kids made fun of his hands. But he hated riding the bus back to his apartment, because he knew what awaited him. He remembers how his father, a preacher, sat watching *Jeopardy* on TV when he came home.

"He'd say, 'So, sugar pudding, God told me what you did in school today, and until you tell me what it was, you'll get beaten every hour on the hour until you tell me.' I would make stuff up. I'd say, 'I pushed kids down the steps,' and he'd say, 'No, that's not what God said.' I would have to go get butt naked, and he'd come into the room with a board to hit me with, and I'd have to stay in my room, while all the other kids were playing around in the apartment. Sometimes it would last all night. At three or four in the morning, I'd be like, 'Oh, I know now.' 'What'd you do at school today?' 'I pushed a kid downstairs and slapped a teacher.' He'd say, 'That's what God told me you did.'"

And Benjamin would get another beating.

"I didn't do none of those things. It was real hard growing up with my family, trying to figure out what God told him. For a long period in my life, I didn't like God. God was lying on me."

At the end of August, the state once again took custody of him from a psychiatric hospital where he was staying, after Camille admitted to officials that if he came home, she would continue to beat him. Benjamin was placed in an emergency shelter, relieved not to be going home. Camille later told her social worker that she had no intention of easing up on her son, saying that if he kept misbehaving, she was going to kill him.

After living in two emergency shelters and a psychiatric ward, a far cry from the nurturing familylike settings that would have served him better, Benjamin went to live at the Mary Lee Foundation's residential treatment center in Giddings, Texas, more than a hundred miles away from his family. Such centers are designed for multiple children, usually those with behavior problems, and have staff members working on a shift basis. They are often locked, and seldom provide the support and affection a youngster could find in a family setting. He was ten.

By phone, his mother told him what to tell workers when they asked about his hands: it was his fault they were burned.

During this period, the state should have been pressing hard either to reunite Benjamin safely with his family or find him adoptive parents. The security that comes from a forever family could have saved him from the years of isolation and heartache to follow. Instead, Benjamin was confined in a residential treatment center for three and a half years—far too long for someone this young—even though the average stay was nine months. Camille's car had trouble making the four-hour round-trip drive to visit him, and she was often forbidden to call him, because her calls and letters upset him. Benjamin's counselors and caseworkers recommended that he be placed in Houston, nearer to his family so that they could go through family counseling together and work toward the possibility of reunification. But caseworkers failed to find an appropriate place for Benjamin within two hours of his family in Houston, the nation's fourth-largest city, and they left only a couple of unanswered messages with his paternal grandparents in Mississippi to see whether they could raise him, rather than going all out to find other adults with potentially strong family ties to him.

The state essentially gave up on Benjamin by the time he was twelve, suffering from post-traumatic stress disorder and reading two or three years behind grade level. "Benjamin's permanency plan is long term foster care," workers from CPS wrote in 1995. "Emancipation/independent living will then be the plan. This is projected to be achieved in 9/2000." Before Benjamin hit his teens, he had already been shuffled through ten different places to live— his grandmother's house, other foster homes, emergency shelters, and three psychiatric hospitals. The agency's plan for permanence simply aimed for more flux, followed by life on his own.

To make matters worse, his mother discontinued the therapy that was provided to help her be a better parent, because her therapist felt that she was making no progress. His father's whereabouts were officially unknown, even after the state subpoenaed him countless times. Benjamin said Claude was living at home, but the state could never find him, likely because Claude did not want to jeopardize Camille's welfare payments for their five children.

Yet even as his parents fell away from their obligation to their son, the state made no effort to find him a new forever home. In the thousands of documents that make up Benjamin's child welfare record, there is no mention of any attempt to find adoptive parents for him. In fact, in his last stint in state custody, in the two years before he turned eighteen, he spent only nine months with foster families, bouncing for the rest of the time among group homes and emergency shelters, less intimate and familial than traditional foster homes. Children are far more likely to be adopted out of foster homes (usually, by their foster parents) than they are from group homes, residential treatment centers, and shelters, where Benjamin spent most of his time as a foster child.

Each time a foster child changes schools, the move can set him or her back four to six months of academic progress. At that rate, how did Benjamin ever progress from one grade to the next? He had never learned to read well, and in seventh grade he still had difficulty telling time. He didn't stay anywhere long enough to make friends or become very involved in sports, activities he would later show great aptitude for, talent that would in several clear ways help save his life.

He missed his brother and sisters and went months without seeing them, even though monthly sibling visits were required under state policy. Once, his mother and his siblings came to visit him, and during a restroom break, his brother showed Benjamin the scars from beatings at home. Benjamin offered to tell his caseworker the next day, but his brother felt that the abuse would just get worse if Benjamin told, so he kept silent. Benjamin knew life in foster care was not a great escape, especially after one of his first foster mothers raped him during a two-month stay. In foster care, survival required tremendous amounts of effort, just as it had at home, but now he was without allies, no brother or sisters to watch his back.

Throughout, Benjamin had few opportunities to feel good about himself and many opportunities to get in trouble. He tested the grown-ups in his various placements, especially any new staff members, and came to like the negative attention he received. It felt good to be punished with words instead of with brute force. He was aggressive with his peers, disrespectful to the staff, and extremely volatile. Time and again, he was kicked out of homes, treatment centers, and classrooms, moving on to the next loveless placement. The pattern lasted his entire childhood. What reason did he have to believe it would change?

Advocates for children have long believed that the Texas child welfare system needs to be improved, and in 2011, the national non-profit legal advocacy group, Children's Rights, filed a federal class-action lawsuit on behalf of foster children against Texas's child welfare system, citing widespread mismanagement. Texas's reported challenges are shared by some other foster care systems across the United States: too many children hover in a parentless netherworld, removed from their birth families and not connected to other kin or a loving adoptive family.

Benjamin had suffered the effects of nearly every flaw in the system described in the lawsuit, even though it was filed long after he was a ward of the state. In Texas, caseworkers have historically worked during the first eighteen months of children's placements either to reunite them with families or to find them different permanent homes with relatives or through adoption. After that period passes, however, the sense of urgency in finding permanent placements often evaporates. The lawsuit cites twelve thousand children frozen in such limbo. In 2009, for instance, sixty-four hundred Texas children had been in foster care for more than three years, bounced through an average of eleven placements, and five hundred children had been in care for more than a decade.

Benjamin had three stints in foster care, during which he lived in almost three dozen different homes, group homes, emergency shelters, residential treatment centers, and juvenile detention centers. He lived in four foster homes from ages two to six, then five congregate care placements in the five years before he turned fifteen, and then an unbelievable thirteen placements—mostly in emergency shelters—in the two years before he aged out of foster care. A state committee studying adoptions found one reason that Texas children were moved so often: poorly supported foster parents were not equipped to handle the trauma many foster children have survived, so they were more likely to lose patience and send children back, usually to a more restrictive setting. In a vicious circle, the children become more traumatized by each upheaval and thus even harder for future foster parents to embrace and adopt.

During his time as a ward of the state, Benjamin's behavior worsened, and he was given more restrictions. He remembers straitjackets, lockdowns, and forced injections of sedatives, and he collapsed into depression and despair. His anger over the abuse and the turmoil, over the lack of something as simple as kindness, rose past the boiling point.

By the time Benjamin reached his fourteenth birthday, in 1996, nothing could contain his temper. That day, as he remembers it, one of his teachers called him dumb, blurting out that he would never amount to anything, and the other kids in the classroom started laughing. It triggered memories from Benjamin's past, of the powerful figure taking unfair advantage. He snapped and threatened to whup the teacher's husband. Even then, he was taller than most of the other kids, madder, and more intimidating. He pushed a computer monitor off the desk. Staff members tackled him and called the police. As he was lying on the ground, being restrained, he threatened to kill the teacher and her husband. He later said it was only the anger talking, but he was charged with "making terroristic threats." He spent months in juvenile detention.

Texas CPS returned Benjamin to his mother's apartment one more time, when he was fifteen. As adolescence set in, Benjamin grew more eager than ever to be accepted. He had never shaken the feeling of being an outcast, and he jumped at the chance to befriend the teenagers of his apartment complex. He conformed to the rules of the neighborhood, heading down treacherous paths, robbing freight trains, piling up stolen beers, cameras, and VCRs in a sheet, and then searching the neighborhood for the local fence. In the end, home became just another layover. When he was taken away from the Bakers for the last time, after a fight with his family that sent him back to juvenile detention, he was shuttled through more than a dozen group settings before he turned eighteen.

A month before that milestone birthday, a psychologist who evaluated Benjamin wrote gloomily about his prospects after foster care, saying that he didn't appear emotionally or functionally ready to live independently. It was "highly questionable" that he could handle stress effectively and follow through on what was expected, and his anxiety threatened to overwhelm him. "He might not be able to handle it," the psychologist concluded.

It's not unusual to experience emotional upset during the transition from foster care to independent living, a period that often brings up unresolved issues from a troubled childhood. Basically, a young person leaving state care needs to re-mourn, and, according to Varda R. Mann-Feder, an associate professor at Concordia University in Montreal, the process can lead to regressive behavior just when new demands hit hardest. Often, the transition comes with rage, noncompliance, depression, and apathy.

WORKING TOWARD MENTAL HEALTH

Some young people end up homeless in part because they have a mental illness that makes it harder to cope with relationships and daily life. Yet the very fact of having no place to live can make even mentally healthy people anxious and depressed and makes those who are unstable even sicker.

Almost 40 percent of the young people at Covenant House have suffered childhood abuse and neglect, which can lead to serious emotional disorders and behavior problems. Many of the young people arriving at our shelters need counseling, medication, or even hospitalization, and they don't have many options for receiving help. In New York City, for instance, the Empire State Coalition of Youth and Family Services reports that there are only twenty-two beds set aside for youth with serious emotional disorders, but more than ten thousand adult beds available city-wide.

Once young people are safe inside, they may resist mental health services. It can be hard for some kids to overcome the stigma of talking to a counselor. "All the kids, when they hear 'psycho-social' or 'counseling,' they think only rich people or crazy people go to counseling," said Vernell Payton, a counselor at Covenant House in Washington, D.C. "I say to them, at some point we all could use counseling."

At the Covenant House Vancouver shelter, eighty young people showing signs of mental health problems were tested in 2007, and the scores showed that the average boy needed hospitalization; the girls were only slightly healthier. Yet the youth had little success connecting with the mental health system, facing six- to nine-month waits for appointments. Even if they made it off the waiting list and went to the nearby community mental health center, they would seldom go back for more appointments, embarrassed by the stigma.

The shelter has since enhanced its staff to include three master's-level clinicians and four social workers, so kids with complex needs who desire counseling or substance abuse treatment can get help on-site. At least one psychiatrist from the Inner City Youth Mental Health

Program works at the shelter Monday through Friday and can see young people in the morning or the evening to accommodate work and school schedules. A psychiatrist is also on call after hours. The average wait to see a psychiatrist dropped from six months to eight days, kids went from keeping half of their appointments to making 80 to 90 percent of them, and over three years, the number of annual hospitalizations from the shelter dropped drastically, from fifteen to three. These in-house services have led to increases in the average stay at the shelter, from only eight days in 2007 to thirteen days in 2010; for kids receiving mental health support, that rose to twenty-one days.

Covenant House has other services for kids with mental health issues, including Arts and Minds, a program at Covenant House Toronto that offers arts, crafts, recreation, and cooking lessons, to help young people with mental health issues build confidence and prepare for work and independent living. Nancy's Place, in Montclair, New Jersey, provides a home to eight young people who need mental health services and transitional living skills. The twenty-four-hour staff includes licensed clinical social workers, and the kids have access to psychologists and vocational specialists. During the course of a recent year, more than half of the young people moved to a more independent living situation, more than half showed greater involvement in work-related activities, and two-thirds showed fewer behavioral issues.

Ready or not, once Benjamin reached eighteen, he'd be on his own, without so much as a high school diploma. He was in plentiful company—as of 2004, less than a third of the nine hundred young people who aged out of Texas foster care had high school diplomas. The problem is typical across the United States. For example, Michigan's reform-minded child welfare director, Maura Corrigan, announced in late 2011 that just over 30 percent of youth who left foster care in the first half of the year had a high school diploma or its equivalent. She launched an aggressive push to increase that percentage, by deploying a team of specialized education planners in fourteen of the state's most populous counties, charged to help such kids stay in school and succeed.

There are currently about four hundred thousand young people in foster care in the United States and sixty-seven thousand in Canada. Life is often gloomy for those who turn eighteen without ever being adopted or fostered in a stable setting. In the United States, 60 percent of the young men who age out of foster care are convicted of a crime by their midtwenties, and three-quarters of the young women are on public assistance.

A 2007 University of Victoria study of young Canadians leaving foster care found that they had fewer years of education and were more likely to rely on income assistance, to have unstable housing arrangements, and to be parents themselves than were young people who had not been in foster care. Researchers found a disturbing correlation between parenting and mental health concerns—young parents who had been in foster care reported depression and anxiety, and most of the young people who had mental health issues were also parents. The report suggested another way of looking at the issue: because young people nationwide are more likely to live with their parents until their late twenties, young people should be considered ready to leave foster care only when they have a mentor, safe and affordable housing, a high school diploma, proper identification, and affordable connections to health and mental health services. Chronological age should not, on its own, determine readiness for independent living.

In Texas, a 2001 study by the Center for Public Policy Priorities surveyed young people who had aged out of, run away from, or quit Texas foster care. Of the thirty young people the researchers could find, eleven were in state prison. The study found that only half of the eligible young people received independent living training from the state, and some said it did not prepare them well for living alone. Almost half of the young people interviewed had health problems, yet almost 60 percent lacked health insurance. More than half had been unemployed or financially unstable.

Benjamin had nowhere to go. He had no place with his last foster family once he turned eighteen, no job, a lousy education, scant skills, and a criminal record, and he knew he could not afford an apartment of his own. In desperation, he even asked Camille whether he could live with her, but she flatly refused. He was scared, in a city where friends were scarce, and fear was scorned.

Luckily, Benjamin's last foster mother took it upon herself to find a place for him once he aged out of the system. She was one of his good foster mothers, he thought. He had lived with her for four months, and she had called him the best foster child she had ever had.

When she brought him to visit the stately, three-story Covenant House shelter in Houston's arty Montrose section, Benjamin worried about the "thuggish mentality" of the young people there who looked at him funny. He tried to act tough to fit in. He withdrew his hands into his pockets, a well-honed instinct to protect himself. He went back to his foster home and tried to eat as much food as possible and lift a lot of weights, so that he could fill out his rangy frame. If he was heading to Covenant House, he wanted to be big and self-sufficient.

Arriving at Covenant House

A few weeks later, a couple pounds heavier, Benjamin stepped through the door of the shelter on his eighteenth birthday, carrying in his misshapen hands everything he owned—two trash bags full of clothes. As he had done on the rough streets of his old neighborhood, Benjamin tried to blend in at Houston's Covenant House. For the first few days there in September 2000, he sagged his pants, trying to be more like his roommate, who had learned from the streets to sleep with a metal pipe under his mattress. Although it looked like a hotel in the Craftsman style, the shelter at first seemed to him like jail. Benjamin felt on edge, so he tried to build his reputation by telling a lie, one that has stuck around for years. He told people he had stabbed a guy sixteen times when in foster care and spent six years in prison for it. It somehow seemed more respectable than the truth.

For most youth at Covenant House, it is not a straight path through the front door to a job, an education, and a lease on an affordable apartment. Some young people stay for a while but rebel against the rules and fail to work toward the goals they set for themselves with the staff. Some are incapable of believing in themselves or in the encouragement of staff members, because all of the grown-ups in their lives have told them they are worthless. For some, it takes many attempts at living indoors before they can trade the freedom and danger of street life for the structure and new expectations of work or school.

Benjamin didn't need to be convinced to work hard, but he came to Covenant House angry, and Todd Mitchell, the first counselor he met, noticed. Mr. Todd served as the director of Rights of Passage, Covenant House's transitional living program. He knew about Benjamin's painful past and watched him closely, taking him under his wing. Benjamin sat for hours in Mr. Todd's office, talking about everything under the sun, gradually opening up. This was something completely new—Benjamin had not trusted an adult in a very long time, not since he last saw his grandmother.

He longed for a father figure, and before long he was working hard to impress Mr. Todd, reaching for the goals they had discussed—finding a job and completing school. Mr. Todd seemed to see the true Benjamin, beyond the scars, beyond the temper. He admired Benjamin's work ethic, his hunger for something more. In three weeks, nearly a record at the shelter, Benjamin had found a job at a supermarket and moved into Rights of Passage.

Yet Benjamin's rage simmered just beneath the surface. One day he became so angry at a boy who was being disrespectful to one of the counselors, he threw him through a wall. Benjamin needed extra guidance when his temper flared, and Mr. Todd was there to help. At first, he tried to teach coping skills, urging Benjamin to count to one hundred when the fury struck. That didn't work so well. Neither did psychological therapy at the shelter—Benjamin had been talking to counselors all of his life and felt that he knew what they wanted to hear.

Mr. Todd decided to take a more direct approach. Benjamin was eighteen now. If he assaulted someone, he'd go to the big man jail, which Mr. Todd described graphically. Mr. Todd saw that Benjamin's tough façade was protecting a scared little boy hiding inside the navy blue nylon jacket he always wore to cover his hands, even when the temperatures climbed. Benjamin's temper was an understandable reaction to the ghosts that haunted and hunted him, the gropings, the schoolyard taunts, the miserable solo walk into each new emergency shelter or group home—Mr. Todd understood that. Menace was Benjamin's mask; it prevented others from seeing his vulnerabilities. Mr. Todd's job was to help the real Benjamin emerge and succeed.

As Benjamin slowly adjusted to life in Rights of Passage, he relied more and more on his counselor to fill the space in his life left vacant by his parents. Mr. Todd used to refer to him as "son," and Benjamin felt privileged. The counselor knew him as no one else did, and he felt as if he could talk to Mr. Todd about anything, even the difficulties of dating while homeless. For the first time in years, change seemed possible.

Benjamin took on two jobs, clocking in at the grocery store in the early afternoon, then working at a pharmacy until seven o'clock in the morning. At night he stocked shelves, sometimes so dead tired he would crouch in the aisle and doze. He had found his jobs with the help of HoustonWorks, a job skills center. One day while Benjamin researched jobs there, an employment counselor affiliated with the Houston Gunners, a semipro football team, approached him. The guy wanted him to join.

For Benjamin, who could finally stay in one place long enough to contribute to a team, it was an astonishing offer. He jumped at the invitation, exhilarated by the chance to earn his place among a group by using his strength and willpower. He threw himself into the arena fully, using the hits and tackles to channel his rage, and the coaches were impressed. They loved the sheer intimidation factor whenever Benjamin walked onto the turf, and the more he played, the more he enjoyed the game, especially tackling.

Between two jobs, football, and studying, Benjamin kept incredibly busy, but he could not outrun the dread and anger that bubbled within him, spilling over unpredictably.

One morning, Mr. Todd, then thirty-four, was driving to work when his pager received a "911" message from the staff at the Rights of Passage apartments. As he sped his green Toyota into the driveway of the slightly rundown brick building, he heard Benjamin storming out the front door.

"What the hell is he going to do? He's not my daddy!" Benjamin shouted in the street.

"Who you talking about?" Mr. Todd asked.

"I'm talking about you," Benjamin replied. Mr. Todd headed inside, where he learned from a coworker that Benjamin had been acting aggressively and not following directions. Benjamin came back inside, interrupting their conversation and walking up to Mr. Todd. The counselor asked a couple of the kids hanging out in his office to clear out, so that he and Benjamin could talk privately.

"You don't tell me what to do," Benjamin said.

"Benjamin, you're in my personal space right now," Mr. Todd said. "Let me be honest, right now, Mr. Todd is feeling threatened."

"You need to feel threatened," Benjamin replied. Mr. Todd told him to pack up his things.

"You're just like my family," Benjamin hollered, cursing, slamming the door and heading upstairs.

It was the worst thing he could have said to Mr. Todd, who knew how badly Benjamin had suffered as a child. He followed Benjamin up the stairs. His colleague asked if he wanted backup.

"No, I got it," Mr. Todd said, and knocked on Benjamin's door. When he heard no reply, he used his key to open the room and found Benjamin cramming the contents of the top drawer of his dresser into a black duffel bag. Mr. Todd called his name, but Benjamin didn't say anything. Instead, he spun around to face Mr. Todd, threatening to hit the counselor if he didn't get out of Benjamin's face. But Mr. Todd, who is six feet tall and stocky, grabbed Benjamin's collar, twisted it, and lifted Benjamin's chin up in the air. It wasn't Mr. Todd's or Covenant House's proudest moment. Benjamin had brought Mr. Todd to the brink, and the counselor had allowed his emotions to carry him when he grabbed the young man. But his words were spot on.

"Don't you ever speak to me like that again," Mr. Todd said. "I'm nothing like your family. I never treated you like your family did, with the horrible things you say they did. I've been here to support you. I love you. I'm going to be here to the very end."

The words washed over Benjamin like the first showers after a Houston drought. Right then, Benjamin broke down and, for the first time in a long while, cried. "I am so sorry," he wept into Mr. Todd's shoulder, "so, so sorry." Mr. Todd held him firmly, shooing away another counselor. After Benjamin apologized to the staff and accepted the consequences for his outburst, he was allowed to stay at Rights of Passage.

Benjamin looked back on the confrontation as a pivotal moment in his life, when he could step away from anger as his default mode for relating to people. The hour that he and Mr. Todd spent talking was a breakthrough. For once, he saw someone stand up to him and stand up *for* him. Someone cared, refusing to pass him along to the next institution. Had Mr. Todd really just said, "I love you"?

"We have to separate the behavior from the kid," Mr. Todd had said. "It's the behavior that's bad, but you're a good kid. You are a treasure."

Even after Benjamin came to understand that Covenant House had his back, he knew he had a steep climb ahead. He asked Mr. Todd to help him finish high school, which seemed almost unthinkable, given the time he had lost. The Houston public schools had labeled him developmentally disabled, with attention deficit hyperactivity disorder. Mr. Todd scheduled some assessments, which revealed that the labels had been wrong, but Benjamin had a lot of lost time to make up. Despite being placed in the tenth grade, he was working on an elementary school level, and he basically could not read.

Mr. Todd encouraged him to enroll in Covenant House's high school equivalency test prep course. If he earned his GED, he would have a shot at a permanent job, maybe even college. Benjamin studied day and night, glad that his roommate worked a night security job and would not be bothered when the lights stayed on late.

Preparing for the reading comprehension section of the test, Benjamin had to read each practice passage up to a dozen times before understanding it, while all of his peers seemed to do so much more quickly. He stormed out after five minutes of working, but his instructor cajoled him back, reminding him of his goal: the diploma. On his days off from work, he studied all day in the Covenant House classroom, then studied more after it closed. He read voraciously and practiced vocabulary, pronunciation, and comprehension. Despite all of his preparations, Benjamin failed the GED test the first two times he took it; the third time, he missed passing it by two points, tantalizingly close.

He knew a verdict had come in. A GED was an emblem of a normal life, an elusive dream that would never be his. He could reach up, time and again, but it would always remain just beyond him. He could hear the whispers in his head—*you're broken, you're mentally retarded, you're dumb.* Mr. Todd watched Benjamin's spirits sink.

If Benjamin did not quite believe in himself, he could not bring himself to disappoint Mr. Todd, and he agreed to try again. In late 2001 he took the test for the fourth time. Days later, to his astonishment, he learned he had passed. That night, the Covenant House staff called Benjamin down to the classroom, where a surprise party awaited him. The floor was covered in red balloons, and he dove into them, overjoyed. He had made up about five years of schoolwork in a single year.

College suddenly seemed possible, and Mr. Todd helped him enroll in a few courses at San Jacinto, a nearby community college. At the end of the semester, Benjamin gave Mr. Todd his first college report card: he had earned a 92—an A—in algebra.

After watching Benjamin's progress in so many areas, Mr. Todd called him into his office one ninety-degree day for a private conversation. He looked down at the raggedy navy windbreaker Benjamin wore all of the time to hide his scars. Its college insignia was fading away after too many washings.

"You know what, Benjamin? You need to stop wearing that jacket," Mr. Todd said. "With the things you are trying to do in your life right now, this is going to be some testimony for some other kids in foster care. Just you wait. You stop covering up your arms and hands, and it will be your testimony for young people in the system."

Benjamin hesitated. The jacket was not nylon to him, it was Kevlar, armor, a shield that kept his hands safe and hidden. But Mr. Todd had not steered him wrong yet. He removed the jacket slowly and balled it up on his lap, with a compliant expression, one that Mr. Todd recognized. In the days afterward, Benjamin hesitated to leave his room without his jacket, but he reminded himself of Mr. Todd's words and strove to honor them. It took several days, but eventually his confidence overtook his embarrassment and he left his room with his arms and hands exposed.

In the spring of 2002, after almost two years at Covenant House, Benjamin realized that he had accomplished most of what he could do there, and it was time to move forward. With three thousand dollars he had saved, he moved into an apartment of his own. He liked being in his own space, free of a curfew. Meanwhile, he was still playing semipro football with the Gunners. Armed with videotapes of his defensive plays, Covenant House helped him get into Cisco Junior College, a two-year school in Abilene, north of Houston, on a football scholarship. As the fall semester approached, he trained hard, trying to prepare for the grueling "two-a-days," the practices before school officially starts.

But he lost his temper at Cisco almost immediately, and his next stop was the bridge by the Houston bus station. Eventually, from there, he saved up enough from his work for the drug dealer to move into one of Houston's YMCAs, where he often worked out. One night, when Benjamin was lifting weights there, a man named Trevor Jefferson overheard him asking another weightlifter for money to buy dinner. That in itself wasn't unusual student behavior, but Benjamin lingered in the weight room as everyone left. Trevor, who worked closely with people at the admissions office at the University of Houston (U. of H.) asked Benjamin who he played football for. Benjamin told Trevor his situation, and Trevor instructed Benjamin to meet him at his office the next morning.

Travis introduced Benjamin around the campus, to the football coach and to people in admissions. With the help of a tuition waiver from the Texas child welfare system, by the end of that day the young man who could barely read a year earlier and was recently living under a bridge was a matriculated college freshman.

He can't explain what pulled him through all of his ordeals. "It just is what it is," he said. "God had a plan. There wasn't anything spectacular that took place, like a falling star or anything. I don't know how I made it this far in life. Here I am, not even believing in myself, that I'd be able to go to college, and He paved the way. God is good. God is great."

U. of H. was "very 'hood" during his time there, Benjamin said, with brawls between the students from Dallas and Houston. No one was quite sure which side Benjamin belonged to, which was just how he wanted it. His old lie about spending six years in prison for stabbing someone came in handy again. The tale grew taller, this time into a murder. Benjamin quickly developed a name for himself on campus, no small feat in a school with almost forty thousand students. A number of fraternities wanted him to join. Young people on the campus whispered, "He just got out of the pen." Benjamin wanted to be that guy, and he became that guy, not the unwanted foster child whose father molested him and whose foster mother raped him. It didn't occur to Benjamin that the horrors he had survived were far worse than jail.

Benjamin spent his first year of college in remedial classes. He couldn't play or practice with the football team until he had earned twenty-four credit hours, but he could lift weights with the other players. His coach said he wanted Benjamin to play defensive end, a position then held by freshman Joey Harrison. The coach told Benjamin to tell Joey he had designs on Joey's position, so Benjamin swaggered up to him and said, "Look, man, you better look out for me, I'm going to play your position. Ain't nothing you gonna do about it, player."

Joey replied, quietly, "Bless you, man, may the best person win. I hope you do well."

Something stirred inside of Benjamin. His fists had been clenched as he approached Joey, but leaving him, Benjamin's hands relaxed. He was struck by Joey's kindness and confidence. Joey had the nickname "Bible Boy," because he carried a Bible everywhere he went, and there was something peaceful about him—one of Benjamin's other friends described him as "dripping with Jesus."

As the fall passed, Benjamin kept observing Joey. In many respects, they were two peas in a pod, both tall, bald, and dark skinned, and obsessed with Cougars pigskin. After a coed embraced Benjamin from behind one evening, mistaking him for Joey, Benjamin told Joey about it on the steps of the library. They laughed, amazed at these brazen college women.

As they talked, Joey asked Benjamin what he planned to do when school closed for Thanksgiving. It was as if a light switch turned off. The joy drained from Benjamin's face, and he averted his eyes. In fact, Benjamin had been dreading the approaching Thanksgiving recess for over a month. He had been hoarding food from the cafeteria for weeks, preparing to hide in a dorm closet, because he had nowhere to go when the residence hall closed.

Joey probed, and, quietly, Benjamin told his story. Joey cried there on the steps and prayed for him, then called his mother,

Clarice Harrison, to see if Benjamin could come home to San Antonio for Thanksgiving. He put them on the phone together.

Mrs. Harrison was all-embracing. There were no unwanted children in her world, no motherless sons. She insisted that Benjamin had Thanksgiving plans, after all.

She and her family drew Benjamin in, claiming him as their son and brother. And from that Thanksgiving break for the rest of the year, Benjamin became a fixture among them. Within no time, Mrs. Harrison invited him to call her "Mom." In fact, when Benjamin mentioned that he didn't even know where his real mother and father were, she contradicted him, surprising him.

"They're right here," she said. During one visit, Mrs. Harrison noticed that Benjamin's hands needed attention. She showed him how to put lotion and grease together, to soften the skin, as she had done for Joey. She told her family that having Benjamin with them was as if their child had been away from home, and God brought him back.

In college that year, Joey often stayed in Benjamin's room, because Benjamin's roommate wasn't around much. Joey coached him on tying a tie and encouraged him to match his clothes and tuck in his shirt. Joey helped him with the correct pronunciation of certain academic terms, and Benjamin, for his part, corrected Joey for showing up to a security guard job in penny loafers, with Bible in hand.

"He helped me be more of myself," Joey said. "And I helped him be more of himself."

As the year progressed, Joey counseled Benjamin about his struggle to form the right kind of intimate relationships with women. When Benjamin first got to college, he had questioned his sexuality: he knew he hadn't enjoyed the sex one of his foster mothers forced on him, and he briefly wondered if perhaps he was gay, because he hadn't fought back when his father molested him. After losing his virginity at twenty-one, he became promiscuous, searching for someone to fix him, as he put it. Joey likened most of Benjamin's girlfriends to convenience stores, when what he really needed, in Joey's view, was to travel the extra mile to find someone who would provide more nutrition for his soul.

Joey encouraged him, understood him, loved him. They were family; Joey felt so, and Mrs. Harrison was sure of it. For Benjamin, used to being a loner, it took a while to see that he was truly part of them, but that feeling grew with time.

"Before anyone can love you, you have to open your heart up to allow them to love you," Mrs. Harrison said. Once Benjamin did so, she felt thankful. "He's making us better people by allowing us to be in his life," she said.

College, for Benjamin, was more than Joey or his family or class or what he said he liked most about it: having a roof over his head and food in his stomach. It was mostly Cougar football, a game that offered him the fellowship of a team and an outlet for his strength and capacity for hard work. Coach LeRoy Smitty, thirty-nine, who was Benjamin's defensive line coach, remembers when Benjamin first joined the team as a sophomore and quickly became one of its stronger, faster, harder-working players. Coach saw in Benjamin all of the intangibles of a Division I, big-time football player—strong as an ox, with no understanding of pain. "What is a sprained ankle when someone is trying to burn you?" coach said, adding that after the abuse Benjamin had survived, "anything that happened on the football field is a piece of cake." Coach taught them to practice the way they played, to give 100 percent, which Benjamin did naturally. But the first year he was eligible to play, Benjamin never got any playing time. Practice *was* his game. He might be big and strong, but he had never played football at this level before, and his knowledge of the game was lacking. "I looked like Tarzan and played like Jane," he said. Yet the coaches kept him on, partly because of the way he goaded his teammates into trying harder.

Benjamin's nerves were part of the problem. He thought too much during scrimmages, afraid of making mistakes. It bugged him that people who did not work as hard as he did played better. At two o'clock practices in the Houston summer sun, he ran some days until he passed out, determined to master the game.

Benjamin finally got his playing time, starting the following year. Joey teased that Benjamin made the all-airport team, that coaches let him off the plane first to intimidate opponents with his size. The team grew to love him. During the annual game with U. of H.'s archrival, Prairie View A&M, Joey sacked the quarterback early on, taking his Cougars to an early lead in a crowded Reliant Stadium. One of Benjamin's teammates started to chant, "B-B, B-B," and soon the whole scarlet-and-white sideline, followed by the U. of H.'s side of the stadium, joined in, demanding some playing time for Benjamin. The coach sent him in, and he sprinted onto the field, a jumble of nerves. In the first play, the quarterback outmaneuvered him with ease.

The Cougars did not set the world on fire in the seasons Benjamin played—going 7–28 from 2003 to 2005. Still, he found that the longer he played football and developed his friendships, the more confident he became. His game-changing sack against McNeese State in 2005 didn't hurt, either. It was a relief to stop trying to fit into anyone else's idea of what he should be—unquestioning son, ex-con, clown, or tough guy.

Yet even as he grew stronger and more self-assured, he was still vulnerable to the pull of the Bakers. Mrs. Harrison remembers visiting Houston and attending a church service in the college gym with her sons. From up in the bleachers, she saw Benjamin talking to two women, one younger, one older. Benjamin stared up at her, looking devastated. When the women turned to look at her, Mrs. Harrison froze. She asked God to forgive her for the rage that flooded her when she realized one was Benjamin's birth mother. Walking toward them, Mrs. Harrison composed herself, prayed for strength, then gave Camille a hug.

When Camille and Benjamin's older sister wanted him to give them a campus tour, he quietly turned aside to Mrs. Harrison and said he did not want to have anything to do with his mother. Mrs. Harrison reminded him about honoring thy father and mother, and he gave the tour, out of respect for his new mother.

Meanwhile, Benjamin's brother, Gamaliel, had started hanging out with him at U. of H., then brought their father to visit, unannounced. Benjamin was livid and wanted to fight, until Joey held him off, telling him he was better than what his father had tried to turn him into.

"You're not a result of what he did to you," Joey said. "You're better than that." Benjamin calmed down, but he needed to stop feeling unsafe and unwell at the thought of his birth family. They were figures from his past, not ever the people he had needed them to be.

In 2006, Joey graduated from U. of H., while Benjamin still had another year to go. His football scholarship had expired, and without Joey's company and the structure of practices and games, he knew he might fall back into the ways of the 'hood. He decided to transfer to Abilene Christian University, a historically black Christian school with about a thousand students. It accepted his credits and let him play two more years of college ball. Benjamin liked the idea of going to school in Abilene, a smaller town six and a half hours from his birth family and the lure of the streets. Even so, he decided to see them one last time before he left Houston for Abilene.

That day, Gamaliel invited Benjamin along on errands but ended up involving him in a crime scene. When Gamaliel asked Benjamin to hold a gun and the drugs he was peddling, Benjamin refused and ended up staring down his brother's rusty .38.

"Blood is thicker than water," Gamaliel told Benjamin. "Nigga, blood is thicker than water," he hissed, implying that brothers should back each other up, or else. "If you're going to be a thug, whatever you want to do with your life, that's fine," Benjamin said. "I want to be the best student and the best football player I'm supposed to be. You be the best thug you can be. You be you. I'll do me. I choose to be a football player and a college student, because I want something out of my life."

He heard the sound of the pistol being cocked.

"You know, I don't even know you," Benjamin replied. "If you're going to shoot, go ahead and shoot, you never have to worry about me again." He turned and walked away, his heart beating rapidly. He walked for about fifteen miles, all the way to campus. It was the last time he saw any of the Bakers.

That day was a crossroads for him. Benjamin saw that he could not help his brother, could not convince him that there was a better way to live. From the time he was eighteen and entering a homeless shelter, sagging his pants, and unable to read, until he was twenty-three and finishing college at a small Christian school, Benjamin had gradually learned to trust others who were on his side and to trust himself to be hard-working, devout, and kind, not the intimidating street tough other people wanted him to be. New people loved him, and, guided by their example, he grew to accept himself. Although he had had ample reasons to be bitter and angry, in five short years, with the help of strong mentors and friends, he had accomplished more than he had dreamed possible.

He graduated from Abilene Christian University in 2008 with a degree in kinesiology, the study of human movement, and a teaching certificate. He earned all As and Bs in the teaching program. He was the first in his birth family to graduate from college.

• • •

It's a Friday night in 2010, Joey is about to graduate with his masters in divinity from Southwestern Baptist Theological Seminary, and Benjamin is hanging out in his friend's nearly empty apartment in Fort Worth, about two and a half hours east of Abilene. Joey will be ordained in a month or so, and once he finishes moving out of here, one of his first official acts will be to baptize Benjamin, immersion-style.

Joey's apartment now has just a desk and a chair, a computer, a smattering of groceries, and a dismantled bed, which will be going home with Benjamin in the Dodge pickup truck he recently bought—Benjamin has been sleeping either on his weight bench or on his floor since he moved in four years ago. While they tell their stories of college life and beyond, Joey sits against the wall by the door. Though he is not carrying his Bible, there is a prim studiousness to him. At first.

Benjamin lounges on the cream-colored carpet, which has ghost prints of the room's missing furniture. He urges Joey to tell about their college years, and the stories, many of them unprintable, flow freely. If Benjamin starts to laugh too hard, he rolls over on his back and spins his legs as if he were bicycle-kicking. At the more outlandish stories, he runs into the bedroom to bend over and belly-laugh.

They are still best friends, brothers. Joey, who is engaged to be married, with Benjamin serving as a best man, struggled for a time to find a balance between the religious teachings he soon would be sharing with others and the women who offered themselves up to a star football player. In divinity school, he decided to fight such temptations and recommitted his body to God and to abstinence. Benjamin had a more difficult time with that, Joey said.

Benjamin recalled that Mr. Todd had noticed his tendency to fall too quickly for women who've been through difficult times. Benjamin struggled with this, knowing that even though he has come this far, there's much more he needs to work on. He has felt an emptiness in many relationships with women, even though there are always three or four who want to date him. Joey feels confident that Benjamin will work through this challenge and points to the way Benjamin talks about lifting weights as a metaphor for life.

Benjamin explained that weight lifting is not optional for him, and the level of effort he puts into lifting sets the bar for his dedication to studying, playing football, and, now, teaching.

"When I go to the weight room, I don't play," he said. "This is my sanctuary." In fact, Benjamin scolds Joey for helping him out too much when spotting him during a lifting session. It reminds Joey of the words of the Negro spiritual: *Lord, don't move the mountain, But give me the strength to climb.*

"That's kind of Benjamin's attitude," Joey said. "He doesn't complain about the mountain in front of him."

The wings of Bolton Middle School in Abilene sprawl for blocks, their concrete walls painted the royal blue of the Vikings and Lady Vikings sports teams, named in a long-ago era when there were more than one or two blond kids in the school. In 2010, almost a quarter of the students are learning English as a second language, all but 4 percent are black or Hispanic, and 85 percent are eligible to receive free or reduced-price lunches. The sidewalks between the wings are roofed, and the young people, some wearing crotch-at-the-knees chinos, some on parole or probation, are bouncing off one another like the atoms they're studying in chemistry. Some cling in pairs, others tumble off the sidewalks like free radicals.

Through these open-air corridors, Benjamin, the school's at-risk coordinator, carries a walkie-talkie in his scarred hands. It summons him from the office to a classroom to the cafeteria, often before he can complete whatever he's doing. He strides fast, past signs that are less common in schools with fewer problems, signs like "Bolton 'Be' Attitudes—Be Respectful. Be Prepared. Be Safe."

The acoustics of the echoing cafeteria make it difficult to pick up his gravelly drawl or the particulars of what the young people whisper to him, about guns or pregnancies or the zeros they are earning in class. As they lean up to him, they almost reach his formidable bicep. Sometimes he has to refer students to the Texas child welfare system, which raised him for half of his childhood. He has always wanted to work with kids, because he understands a lot of what they're going through and wants to protect them.

His answer to most people—a waitress or a coworker, a helpful student, a rebellious one—is an even-toned "I appreciate you." And when it's time to change classes, he heads down the halls with what seems like the only sense of urgency around.

"You're not walking like a winner," he says to one kid.

"What am I going to say?" he asks another student, who immediately remembers the school rule and tucks the navy polo shirt of his school uniform into his khakis.

"You're a mind reader," Benjamin replies.

Scanning their expressions and body language, he picks up subtle signals, a deep slouch here and lowered eyes there. He notes one sad-looking girl and says he will check in with her later, when she is no longer surrounded by girlfriends. He takes another downcast young man off for a walk-and-talk around the edge of the school driveway.

When it turns out that this eighth grader has some serious troubles, Benjamin lets the school counselor know. The parents are called in, and the youngster goes to a treatment program for the counseling he needs. Because they have a relationship, the boy can tell Benjamin something he won't tell his counselor, that he is depressed because of a girl.

Benjamin has spoken softly to students who are abused or pregnant, who have run away from home, even those who are suicidal. He considers his hands the tools that sometimes help him reach the kids in trouble. He grabs their attention and eventually

their trust by recounting why his hands are splotchy, the skin looking weathered and elderly in places. "I tell them I had a hard life,"
he said. "I don't even have to verbalize it, they can see it. They say
'Man, for real?' Their lives haven't been a crystal stair. They get it. I
really feel that kids can relate after I explain to them, like they feel
like I'm on the same page. It's a blessing, what the job has given me
the opportunity to do. I'm blessed, and I know that."

He uses his hands, but it is never easy, nothing he does flip-
pantly. Sometimes, when talking to young people he doesn't know
very well, he just tells them he was reaching for wieners on the
top of the stove, making a joke about his famously large appetite.
It hurts to say his mother burned him. He never lives it down, he
said. He has gotten used to how the backs of them look, but he still
tries to hide the scars on the inside of his left hand.

These two particular school days in 2010 are quiet by his standards, with no bloodshed, two suicidal students, five Latino kids
suspended at once for cutting class and lying about it and calling Benjamin a racist for sending them to the office, a girl telling
him not to talk to her with his "bald-ass head," a rough dismissal
that led him across the street to disperse kids, and a Latino boy
calling him a "ho-ass nigger"—relations between Hispanics and
blacks in the school are complicated and often result in big fights.
Throughout, Benjamin listened to hundreds of voices, giggles and
taunts, and tall tales from kids who told him that actually they were
not late to class, they did *not* throw gang signs or the piece of paper
everyone saw them throw, they do *not* know their phone number or
address or father's cell number or whether their mother still works
at McDonald's. The lies fall out of their mouths like clowns from a
circus car, but in the face of such exasperating behavior, Benjamin
remains calm, removed now from his days as a teenage powder
keg. When they poke and prod him, rough-housing and trying to
get a rise out of him, he occasionally bear-hugs one who gets too
rough, but he always keeps his cool.

In every single child at Bolton, he sees himself, young and powerless, trying to make sense out of the cruelties of broken families, beaten-down caregivers, drugs, mental illness, grinding poverty, and violence.

Many afternoons, Benjamin visits the students' homes, to talk to the families and let them know of any problems at school. There, he views the students' economic conditions close up. In some of the dark, crowded apartments he visits, there isn't room for two people to sit down. He often lived better as a ward of the state and has come to believe that poverty is a main cause of the behavior problems he sees in many kids at Bolton—it stresses them out and keeps them from functioning at their best.

His first year at Bolton, Benjamin had an idea to help individual students who were struggling in school and needed real motivation. Although his long-term substitute's salary left him stretching to pay his bills, he promised his students twenty dollars for every A they earned. At the end of the marking period, he ended up spending well over a thousand dollars for the As the students brought him. Yet his whole paycheck was worth their trust. He knew he'd lose the kids if he went back on his word. The teachers and the principal wondered aloud if he was out of his mind.

"Probably so, but the kids still learned, and I learned. I learned not to do that anymore," Benjamin said, laughing.

He's looking forward to pursuing a master's degree and eventually become a school principal. He would like to run a school of last resort for kids with behavioral problems. He wants them to have someone to trust. And he would make sure that it is beautiful, so that the young people know they are valued.

Coach Smitty, Benjamin's mentor from U. of H., is glad to know that his former defensive end is choosing a career helping young people, because he can reach them in a way few others can. "There's no class, no psychological evaluation, or rash of theories that would help you be able to reach some of these kids, if you don't have street savvy, if you've not been there when the lights are off and your mom is beating you and you don't know where your next meal is coming from, and you're getting hit and you don't know why," Coach Smitty said. "He could reach those kids. Benjamin found out he was stronger than what he thought. I think he had the right people around him, and that just went a long way."

Fixing Foster Care

—Kevin Ryan

During my years as head of New Jersey's child welfare reform effort, and through my work supporting other reform efforts in Michigan, New York, Oklahoma, and Washington, D.C., I have seen states struggle to reduce the number of young people who leave foster care at ages eighteen to twenty-one without a family to call their own. Despite significant state and federal investment in reforms during the last decade, this seems to be one of the toughest nuts to crack. The failure to solve this problem is a major reason we see so many homeless young people at the doors of our Covenant House shelters. If we could win one battle in the war to prevent our kids from becoming homeless, this is the one I would choose.

Most children—78 percent in 2010—exit foster care to a safe, permanent family: their birth parent, a relative serving as a legal guardian, or through adoption. (Another 8 percent leave to live with relatives who are not their legal guardians, who sometimes, but not always, provide a permanent home.) But 11 percent of the children leaving foster care age out of the system with no place to go. That's nearly twenty-eight thousand teenagers, up sharply from a little more than twenty thousand a decade earlier. There's no clear consensus about the cause of this increase, which comes even as the overall number of children in foster care decreased 26 percent since 2000. Some states have a much more serious problem than others—in Virginia, for example, almost a third of youth who exit from foster care do so without a family in place.

Turning eighteen doesn't suddenly give young people new skills or power; it simply leaves many from the child welfare system with no home and no support system. Without that safety net, many former foster youth struggle, at great cost to themselves and society. Most youth need their families' support long after that milestone birthday, and for many alumni of foster care, the most essential tasks—completing school, finding work, saving, and knowing how to shop, cook, and pay the rent—remain elusive puzzles.

Their disadvantages extend beyond the classroom. A 2005 study by the University of Chicago's Chapin Hall showed that former foster youth in Iowa, Illinois, and Wisconsin were twice as likely as other youth to report that they lacked enough money to pay for rent and utilities, and sometimes even food. Fewer than half of the twenty-three- and twenty-four-year-olds in the study who had aged out of foster care in 2004 held a job in 2010, and most who did were not earning a living wage. Nearly four out of every ten of these young people had been homeless at one point since leaving foster care. Given the correlation between leaving foster care without a family and unemployment, incarceration, and unplanned pregnancy before age twenty-one, a 2009 report funded by Jim Casey Youth Opportunities found that the young people who age out of foster care each year cost $5 billion in additional costs to government and individuals for welfare and Medicaid expenses, the costs of incarceration, and lost wages and tax revenues. That price, on a human as well as fiscal scale, is far too high.

Finding a permanent family for foster children, especially older ones, is a tall order of child welfare leadership. Teenagers are generally less likely than younger foster children to be placed with a family who might adopt them, and of all the kids reunified with their families or adopted into new ones, only a small fraction are teenagers. The challenge has led to boldness and innovation in some quarters. Focusing on the foster children who have been waiting for homes the longest, Wendy's Wonderful Kids, a program of the Dave Thomas Foundation for Adoption, awards grants to public and private adoption agencies to hire adoption professionals to recruit adoptive families aggressively. The program has paved the way for almost three thousand adoptions in the United States and is growing steadily.

In New Jersey in 2007, the child welfare system I led devoted its most experienced staff members to finding permanent homes for the one hundred foster children who had been waiting the longest. We placed half of the children within eighteen months, so youth who had waited as long as twelve years were finally connected with families, including in some instances extended relatives. In St. Louis, a program called Extreme Recruitment has used retired detectives and child-welfare workers to locate dozens of relatives for young people stuck in foster care, finding permanent homes for 70 percent of them, compared to 40 percent under standard procedures. A federally funded evaluation of the project will help determine how effective it can be on a broader scale.

To help kids in foster care leave for permanent homes and achieve better outcomes, the U.S. Congress unanimously passed the Fostering Connections to Success and Increasing Adoptions Act of 2008, which offers states federal matching aid if they choose to provide assistance to relatives who become legal guardians of foster children. States can also receive federal matching money if they let young people stay in foster care up to the age of twenty-one, as long as they are in school, working, or engaged in other constructive activities. For example, the Texas legislature in 2009 authorized the extension of the state foster care program under these circumstances, as did the Michigan legislature in 2011. Yet as of February 2012, just slightly more than half of the states had successfully applied for federal matching dollars to expand guardianship care, and only eleven had received federal approval for matching aid to extend foster care to age twenty-one. More states need to join in these efforts, to help the children they have taken in. When they do, the results are promising: one study of young people in Illinois who could stay in foster care until age twenty-one showed they were three times more likely to complete at least one year of college and 38 percent less likely to become pregnant, compared to young people who left care at eighteen.

Particularly in difficult economic times, government leaders and advocates need to think creatively. Given limited government resources and the growing stock of abandoned, bank-owned properties across the United States, it makes sense to imagine a new way to develop safe housing opportunities for vulnerable youth. Federal policymakers should encourage banks, perhaps with tax incentives, to contribute foreclosed properties to nonprofit organizations without liability, relieving the banks of the responsibility of maintaining these structures. The White House could then target to nonprofit groups a number of existing federal Section 8 housing vouchers from the U.S. Department of Housing and Urban Development, for use by youth aging out of foster care. Rather than becoming eyesores in their neighborhoods, these vacant houses can become homes for young people who desperately need them. The program would promote the growth and redevelopment of struggling communities, while allowing youth to prepare for independent living in a safe and stable setting. The idea involves the type of innovative partnership among child welfare nonprofits, banks, and federal agencies that too rarely occurs. It's a cost-effective strategy to expand the safety net for young people aging out of foster care.

Another crucial way to improve foster care is to reduce the number of times children move from caregiver to caregiver. When children bounce among placements, as Benjamin did more than thirty times, how can they form the kind of enduring attachments that help them become self-assured and trusting? Many wander through childhood believing there is something wrong with them, leaving scars on their hearts and minds that last a lifetime. When children move too often, their health care is disrupted and their health suffers, their education lags, and their roots wither, as connections with siblings and other birth family members weaken.

When a child welfare system aims for stable placements, that overriding goal actually helps it meet other goals as well. In 2007 in New Jersey, with our eyes on the prize of fewer moves for kids, we knew success meant stability for children, and stability often meant educational achievement, better health care, and stronger connections with caregivers, who could become forever families, if necessary.

Research shows the importance of placing children with relatives whenever safe and possible. A far-reaching study initiated in 2006 by the Children's Hospital of Pennsylvania followed a large group of young children entering the Philadelphia child welfare system and revealed that they typically found more stability when placed with relatives. One ringing achievement of the federal Fostering Connections law is that many of these relatives can now become permanent guardians without forfeiting state assistance, a development likely to bolster stability and permanency, especially if more states get on board.

Although strong and supportive child welfare systems are desperately needed, we can't forget that whenever it is safe for children to stay home, they should. Anyone who has watched a caseworker forcibly separate a child from a parent knows what heartbreak looks like. Children very often do better living with their own families with the proper support systems in place than they do with strangers in foster care. It is important to note that of the cases that child welfare workers investigate, most do not involve abuse and neglect. Many arise because of the cascading consequences of poverty—the need for groceries, utility aid, shelter, or child care, for instance. The trauma of being removed from families, friends, schools, and familiar surroundings cannot be underestimated, and none of it happens by accident. Billions more dollars have been spent on the machinery of foster care than on safely preventing admissions to foster care. Programs that supply wraparound services, such as Memphis's Youth Villages Intercept, for example, remain more the exception than the rule, even though they have helped young people with behavioral or emotional problems stay in their homes, by providing family therapy and parenting skills, at a lower cost than foster care.

A growing movement, begun in the early 1990s but under way currently in fewer than twenty states, has created a "differential response" system, one that seeks to address families' social needs when child abuse and neglect are not suspected, even though concerns about the family have been reported to a state child abuse hotline. The millions of calls received by these hotlines annually vary in severity. For example, an isolated worry about children sleeping in a hot attic bedroom in the summer is not comparable to a call alleging that a parent repeatedly leaves an infant unattended, and neither is akin to allegations that an adult beats or sexually exploits a child. Yet in most state child welfare systems, there is a uniform reaction to all of these calls: an investigation of the family to determine whether child abuse or neglect has occurred. Differential response embraces the idea that a traditional investigation is not appropriate in all cases. Maybe the family simply needs an air conditioner.

Consider the homes without electricity or heat in the wintertime; the single parent with two jobs and no child care; the family with a sick parent and a truant child. Few would argue that children in such homes need to be pulled from their families, which may just need heating assistance, subsidized child care, or Meals-on-Wheels to stay together safely. Different families need different kinds of help, which can include behavioral health assistance, groceries, transportation, or access to local health care. Any of these services costs significantly less, in dollars and heartache, than removing children to foster care.

Research shows that families receiving assessments of their needs and strengths, rather than investigations, are more likely to engage in solving their problems and accept help, which makes sense. It is far easier to welcome social workers at your door if they are offering you help that you need, rather than threatening to take away your children.

In many cases, differential response can assure children's stability and well-being in their own homes, promote healthy family functioning, and prevent child abuse and the need for foster care. It also provides families with an established network of formal and informal supports. Several states—Texas among them—have conducted evaluations of their differential response systems, and the results are encouraging: children are less likely to be the subject of subsequent maltreatment allegations, and families are more likely to be preserved safely.

Mental health services, including counseling and respite care, must be more readily available to people such as Benjamin's mother, those at high risk of abusing children. Until parents, particularly impoverished ones, have access to mental health or addiction services, their children will continue to live in danger. Child protection agencies need to ensure that parents can find help, said Robert N. Davison, the executive director of the Mental Health Association of Essex County, New Jersey. He also suggests that community members need to reach out to neighbors who may be struggling with mental illness, in the way they would help a parent with a physical injury or illness. The stigma surrounding mental illness keeps people—many of them parents—from getting help. Their children suffer as a result. In addition, the need for mental health services for current and former foster children is vast and unmet.

For young people such as Benjamin who do "graduate" from foster care, without a party or a diploma, a thin network of youth shelters and transitional living programs may be available to help them establish safe and stable lives on their own. Congress enacted the Runaway and Homeless Youth Act in 1974 to fight youth homelessness with street outreach to help kids come in off the streets; crisis shelters where children and youth can find a safe place to stay; and transitional living programs, such as Covenant House's Rights of Passage program, to give young people the basic skills they need to learn how to live safely and independently. Federal funding for transitional living programs covers only about four thousand youth a year, just one in seven of those who age out of foster care, and most programs have long waiting lists. Charities such as Covenant House, relying substantially on private donations, strive to fill the gap, but the need is enormous.

4

A Homeless Teen Mother Reaching for a New Life

Creionna's Story

How do you know how to mother, if you haven't been mothered yourself? Like a bird that can somehow build a nest without having seen it done before, Creionna made the hardest decision of her life to protect her child. She left home with her six-week-old son and headed to a homeless shelter. She felt that her family would only subject him to the pain and neglect she had felt after her mother died and her father went to prison. She wanted her son to know the stability she'd always craved.

Your average teenager doesn't know this. Say you get pregnant or get someone pregnant, and you have a baby. Nearly 750,000 American teenage girls do, every year, a third of them under eighteen. Almost 90 percent of teen mothers are unmarried. You need a place to live, but to afford your average two-bedroom apartment, you need a job that pays $18.46 an hour. To afford that apartment on a minimum wage, you need to work more than twenty hours each weekday. And to keep that job, you have to find child care, but in thirty-six states, a year of child care costs more than a year in a state college. And, of course, child care for those twenty-hour days would cost much more.

What happens if you're a homeless teen parent? You have an even steeper climb to reach independence. You've undoubtedly experienced some significant rift with your family, and you probably have the attendant psychological burdens, not to mention sleep deprivation from the baby and from worrying. Families are rejected from adult homeless shelters almost a third of the time, and the average wait for a federal housing voucher is thirty-five months.

Covenant House was able to serve 871 young mothers (and their 947 children) in the United States in 2010. About 87 percent of the mothers were unemployed, compared to 70 percent of other Covenant House youth. Young parents are also less likely to have a high school diploma or its equivalent, making a job search even more difficult. Soon, that job, the apartment, and dreams of independence recede into the future. You're struggling for two, and you are running out of options. It's no wonder up to 80 percent of homeless teen mothers cannot find a stable place to live long term.

If there were more song lyrics accurately describing the life of a teen mom, instead of glamorizing the life of a pimp, more teens might know about the difficulties of parenting. But your average kid just doesn't.

Say you beat all of the odds, finish high school, get a job, find an affordable apartment that rents to people with no rental history, scrounge together the first- and last-month's rent, and, wanting the best for your child and yourself, you want to go to college. Your day would look something like that of Creionna, a young mother who grew up in poverty along the Gulf Coast of Louisiana. Your day would start at five forty-five in the morning, would require seven bus or street car rides, and would end between seven and eight o'clock at night, just in time to make dinner and start doing homework. Creionna falls to bed exhausted every night.

For Creionna, a motherless mother and a hurricane refugee, the struggle for independence was complicated further by geography—in post-Katrina New Orleans, most affordable apartments have been destroyed, forcing rents up by 50 percent on average. Her family, such as it was, had scattered. The grandmother who had raised her now lived in a nursing home, and her father watched her walk out one night with her six-week-old baby after a bad fight.

That baby, Dominic, has become her inspiration, the reason she works her heart out. Jim Kelly, the lanky, warmhearted founder and executive director of Covenant House New Orleans, has seen this happen many times, as young parents kicked around by life insist on protecting their kids with a passion.

"Our children are often pushaways or throwaways, and sometimes it makes them—depending on the DNA of the young mother—fierce advocates. They say, 'I'm not going to throw my child away, or pass my child off, the way that happened to me.'"

Covenant House's hope is to break the patterns that some social scientists see—abused and neglected children going on to abuse or neglect their own children, and children of teen mothers growing up to become teen parents. The staff works hard with young parents to teach them the skills and the patience necessary for the hardest job on earth—raising a thriving child.

From the bottom of a dark, musty closet piled high with everyone else's clothes, nine-year-old Creionna could hear her aunts, cousins, and grandmother talking raucously about what they would do once they won the lottery. For more than an hour, she stayed in the back room of her grandmother's shotgun house, holding a big kitchen knife against her bare belly, wishing she had the courage to push it through.

She was done. Didn't want to live anymore. Didn't want to be the motherless girl who didn't get a birthday cake, the girl whose grandmother threw out the one new party outfit she'd ever received. Didn't want to be the one whose people sent her out alone to "make groceries," as they say in New Orleans, and cart them back five blocks in the swampy summer heat. Didn't want to be the kid with the "messed-up grill," the broken front tooth that was never fixed after she'd fallen last year in school. All of the kids made fun of her; third grade was misery. She dreamed of joining Dominique, her pretty young mother, in heaven.

Dominique had died at twenty-one, when Creionna was just two. Her heart was too big; that's what Creionna's grandmother, Tasha, said. Creionna had no memory of her mother and just one photograph. In it, Dominique wears long earrings and a beaming smile, holding her pudgy infant proudly, a bouquet in a beauty queen's arms.

Creionna's father raised her after her mother's death, while her brother, then seven, went to live with Tasha. But when Creionna was seven, her father went to prison for selling drugs, and she joined her brother with their grandmother, who became Creionna's legal guardian. At any time, up to ten people lived in the cramped three-bedroom house, mostly aunts and cousins.

Creionna hoped that Tasha might love her extra after Dominique's death—after all, Creionna was her daughter's daughter—but the opposite seemed true. Tasha barely spoke to her, and when she did, say, to give her a shopping list, her voice was seasoned with dislike. Come report card time, Creionna's cousins won dollars from their grandma for their Cs and Ds, like beads tossed from Mardi Gras floats. But Tasha gave Creionna nothing for her better grades. When an uncle took to mocking Creionna and punching her in the face, Tasha did nothing to stop him.

Creionna quickly understood that she could not lean on her grandmother. Around this time, Tasha sent her on the bus to buy crawfish one afternoon. On the way to the bus stop, Creionna saw a man acting like something was wrong with his car. As she approached, he exposed himself to her, and she ran from him, furious. She returned home in a sweaty panic, out of breath, but Tasha had only one thing on her mind: where were the crawfish?

Eventually, Creionna tried as best she could to avoid home and began to spend more time with her brother and his friends. When the father of one of those boys took a special interest in her, luring her into a dark room in his house and fondling her, she felt more alone than ever, without anyone to turn to for help.

The night in 2000 when Creionna sat with the knife against her stomach, her family didn't win the lottery. Creionna stayed in Tasha's closet, puzzling over them. What caused her grandmother to hate her so? Was it because she hadn't liked Creionna's mother, or, as Tasha said, because Creionna cried a lot as a baby and didn't seem to like Tasha? Was it resentment over having another mouth to feed? Was it Creionna's darker skin, a milk chocolate hue that made her grandmother favor some of the house's lighter-skinned relatives? Or was it something else? Creionna sat there wishing someone would come looking for her and give her the answer. When she left the closet, no one had even noticed her absence.

Creionna moved back in with her father, who had recently been released from jail, when she was thirteen. Not long afterward, Tasha suffered a heart attack and a stroke that left her partially paralyzed and unable to care for herself, so Creionna moved back to help care for her and tend to the chores. The house, always the place where relatives flopped if they had nowhere else to turn, quickly sank into filth and mayhem without Tasha at the helm. It fell to Creionna, still the lowest ranked among them, to clean up their mess and evict the maggots. She did her best to scour, scrape, and scrub, but it was as pointless as sandbagging when the levees broke. When her grandmother moved to a nursing home, Creionna returned to live with her father.

She had just started tenth grade in a program that would have let her graduate with college credits when Hurricane Katrina flooded New Orleans, killing more than nineteen hundred people, causing $81 billion in property damage, and washing away the hopes of many of its residents. One of her friends died in the flood-waters, trying to rescue his sister. Countless others lost everything they owned. Suddenly, virtually everyone in her life was either homeless or out of work. Dirty water buried her world.

HOMELESSNESS IN NEW ORLEANS

—Kevin Ryan

I am standing at the site where, three days after Christmas 2010, eight young people died in an abandoned warehouse in New Orleans's Ninth Ward. It was a brutally cold night, and homeless men, women, and children across the city were scrambling for warmth. In the warehouse, young people burned trash in a barrel to keep warm, and the structure caught fire shortly before two o'clock in the morning.

Jonathan Guerrero, who had just turned twenty, was one of them. His friends described him as a lovable guitar-ist who enjoyed playing for the many tourists in the city's French Quarter. Originally from Texas, Johnny quit college and his job and became a traveler, jumping freight trains, answering to the street name "Carwash," and finding hope in his music. He didn't put enough money together to pay rent every month, so he squatted in empty buildings, doing the best he could to survive.

Seventeen-year-old Melissa Martinez was a great animal lover. She dreamed that one day she'd leave her part-time waitressing job and travel overseas to lead an animal rescue mission. Melissa had big dreams, just like her friend Katie Simianer, twenty-one, who worked hard to earn a welding certificate in her Job Corps program and was actively looking for work in the trades. These kids had plans.

But that December night, as the temperature suddenly fell below freezing, talk of the future took a backseat to their urgent need to sleep inside. Johnny, Melissa, Katie, and several of their friends found an empty corrugated metal and wood warehouse abandoned after Hurricane Katrina and made their way inside. They lit their fire, huddled together, and drifted off to sleep. The carbon monoxide from the open fire poisoned them, and when the drum tipped over and ignited the warehouse, Johnny, Melissa, Katie, and their friends never woke up.

The following March, a weathered memorial sign still sits in place of the demolished warehouse at the corner of St. Ferdinand and North Prieur Streets. It overlooks a small collection of memorials—a teddy bear, some cards, some long-wilted flowers, a cross, and a faded photo of one of the boys—the only evidence that young people died there.

Although many of those who died were visitors from out of town, most people who still find shelter in New Orleans's abandoned buildings are hurricane survivors. Like the buildings they inhabit, they are beaten but not destroyed. The storm took out 72 percent of New Orleans's housing stock, and almost fifty-two thousand rental units were seriously damaged or destroyed. Not surprisingly, there were 70 percent more homeless people in New Orleans in 2011 than prior to the storm, for a total of about sixty-five hundred people. At the same time, the number of emergency shelter beds has declined by more than a third, from about 870 to 550, and Covenant House New Orleans remains the only shelter for homeless teenagers.

Covenant House New Orleans served slightly fewer than sixty young people each night at the time of the storm, but more than a hundred young people six years later. The charity's founding executive director, my friend Jim Kelly, thought much about the challenges confronting homeless youth in New Orleans after the warehouse fire. "The kids who walk though our doors each night come from all different backgrounds. Some, like the traveling kids who were killed in the fire, stop by for a sandwich, a shower, and clean clothes, but only a few are willing to stay and let us really help them," he said.

"Some, like the more classic runaways, if we get to them soon enough, are easy to assist in getting back home. But the majority of our kids come from dysfunctional and abusive homes. You have to remember that our kids were eleven, twelve, and thirteen, the tween years, when Katrina hit. Their already upside-down lives soon spiraled out of control."

Yet there is good news, too: the homeless population has decreased by 12 percent since 2009, largely due to 441 new affordable supportive housing units and a rapid rehousing program for evicted people, funded by federal and local stimulus dollars. Much is still to be done, but the people of New Orleans are indomitable and inspired. Like the kids who fill our shelter each night, they are unbroken.

Creionna and her family had escaped ahead of the monstrous storm, getting stuck in traffic for what felt like a day, sleeping in their car in front of a packed hotel. They avoided the worst of the hurricane in Waterproof, Louisiana, population 834, about two hundred miles north. From there, Creionna ached whenever she saw television images of her nearly drowned hometown. Her family eventually settled in another rural town, and her father sent her to a school with only about a hundred kids, fifteen of them from New Orleans. But Creionna hated living in the country, and after a few months, with her father's blessing, she returned to New Orleans to live with a maternal aunt. That worked, until the house became the family's new base camp for various relatives with drug problems. One aunt had a habit of stealing and wearing Creionna's far-too-small clothes, while an uncle stole some of her remaining outfits and sold them for his next fix. At fifteen, Creionna felt like the only responsible adult in the house.

There was one bright spot—a young man named Rashad lived next door. Creionna found him handsome—she had a weakness for dreadlocks—and she liked that he was stubborn, similar to her. They both had crazy families, a cause for commiseration. Rashad listened to her talk about her life as they sat up on the fire escape, and he added his own horror stories. After dating for six months, she became "with child," as she calls it. Deep in denial, Creionna hid her pregnancy for five months. Her neighbors believed that drinking a capful of bleach would cause a miscarriage, so she considered doing that or killing herself. When friends asked her whether she was pregnant, she said no and asked what made them think she was. "That big stomach," they replied.

When people looked down their noses at her and asked her why she let herself get pregnant so young, she had no idea what they were talking about. "I didn't have a mother," she said. "I had nobody to guide me. I was on my own."

When Creionna was about twenty weeks' pregnant, her aunt figured it out and called her father, who was furious. He came to the aunt's porch and told Creionna she had to have an abortion, but she said it was too late. They fought and he hit her hard, in the chest. She fell back, unsure whether he was trying to make her miscarry but unwilling to test him. She started to cry, and watched him leave in a fury.

Rashad, meanwhile, also voted for an abortion and denied that the baby was his. Their relationship quickly went south. She watched him hustle the neighborhood, bedding a slew of girls, running hard from any responsibility. Sixteen and pregnant, she became ever more isolated, a loner, angry at herself for ending up in this position. Her anthem was the Ludacris song "Runaway Love," about a pregnant girl everyone abandons, who flees home. She listened to it over and over on the radio or on MTV, and it made her cry every time. *This isn't happening to me*, she thought.

Meanwhile, life at her aunt's became unbearable. Creionna worried that if she remained in the midst of her family's pervasive drug use, the police would inevitably come in and take her baby from her. She was earning about $150 a week at McDonald's, paying for her own school uniforms and waking herself up for school. Meanwhile, she saw her cousins selling drugs and earning $1,000 a week. *These people are mean, dangerous, and crazy*, she thought. *They're not taking me down.* The moment her water broke, she left for the hospital and never set foot in the house again.

In the spring of 2007, Creionna, who had just turned seventeen, labored alone while her dad, stepmom, and aunt stayed in the waiting room. After an emergency C-section, she looked down at her son. True to the neighborhood superstition, the baby looked exactly like the person she loathed the most—herself. She named her mirror-faced boy Dominic, after her mother. Cradling her infant son in the hospital, Creionna did not recover quickly. The doctors never figured out why her blood pressure and pulse remained so high for more than a week. She chalked it up to stress and went back to her father's, to start life as a new mother.

Nothing had prepared her for this new responsibility, not even all of those years taking care of Tasha and picking up after her relatives. When Dominic cried, his eyes squinting tears, his voice filled her father's house with helplessness. She wanted to give up—it was too hard, and she didn't know what she was doing. Dominic's frustrated wailing regularly woke up her father and her stepmother, and they were livid if she let the baby cry too long. She didn't know how to calm him or them. She hoped her father could give her some guidance on how to handle the baby, but he put his wife, who had no experience with infants, in charge. Failing the baby was not an option—Creionna couldn't turn her back on her son and let anyone else raise him. She had known that fate and hated it. She would not let it be Dominic's.

It was after nine o'clock and the Walmart had closed for the night. Creionna had thought she could catch a bus somewhere, but the buses stopped running at eight in this New Orleans suburb where her father had settled. She had her six-week-old son, a well-stocked diaper bag, the clothes she wore, and no destination.

She was undone from trying to finish the school year, relying on her stepmother and cousin, among others, as sitters most days of the week. She had heard her father and stepmother trying to teach her son to say "mama" and "dada" to them and couldn't stand the thought of them taking him from her and raising him as their own. She didn't want her child to experience the chaos and neglect that colored her childhood and left her wanting to die before it was half over. Her father and stepmother had ganged up on her with predictions of how she would be like every teenage mother and leave her baby with them while she ran the streets. And now, her father's words were fresh in her memory, about how she wasn't worth the trouble.

In the steamy parking lot, Creionna started to cry. She was rattled by a pounding chest and had been losing clumps of hair. She couldn't stay at her aunt's, because that house was overrun by a steady stream of drug customers. Her grandmother disliked her and in any event was incapacitated, and her baby's father was no help. Creionna was too old for foster care. She watched cars full of happy-looking families pull out of the store's lot, which would soon be empty, except for the young mother and child.

An elderly couple approached and asked her what was wrong. Right there, she made what she calls the hardest decision of her life. She asked them to take her to Covenant House New Orleans, a shelter she had heard about in school months earlier. She had walked over to North Rampart Street, on the edge of the French Quarter, to check out the three-story brick building the outreach workers had described during their visit to the school cafeteria. As she walked by it, the young people hanging out along the sidewalk, near the arching palm trees, made her think twice.

Oh my God, that can't be me, she thought. *That's for dirty kids.* But tonight was different. Her baby was restless, and she couldn't take him home. She didn't have one.

The ride to the city lasted about half an hour. The couple gave her forty-five dollars to help. She wished she had written down their names, to thank them, to pay them back. But they were kindly ghosts, gone.

Arriving at Covenant House

She sat in a small counselor's office lined with lockers, answering questions about her life, lulling her baby, glad for the air conditioning but embarrassed at how sadly typical she sounded. Like many homeless young people in New Orleans, Creionna had no high school diploma, no monthly income, no food stamps, no official identification, no other relatives she could live with, plus a baby. She also had a history of physical, sexual, and verbal abuse; no mother; and no work history, aside from her few months at

McDonald's, which ended as Dominic's birth approached. She didn't even list herself as the head of her own household—that honor went to Rashad, her baby's father, and they had broken up almost a year ago. She listed her primary caretaker as her grandmother, who was in no position to take care of her.

Despite all of this, Creionna did have an edge over many of her peers, even though she could not see it at the time. She had stayed off the streets. She had not resorted to survival sex or prostitution, and she did not have a criminal record. She had finished eleventh grade. Even though she believed her family was crazy and the majority were drug dealers or addicts, she was not mentally ill and had not abused drugs.

The baby was tired and hungry, and so was she. Creionna followed the counselor just a few steps into the dining room, and the shelter's cook, Gail Singleton, nearly sixty, warmed up some leftovers from the evening's supper for her. Ms. Gail, who pinned her hair up in a French twist and wore colorful scrubs like those favored by pediatric nurses, had seen this all too often: an exhausted teenager with no place to go and a needy infant in tow. Creionna accepted the food with a small murmur of thanks and not much eye contact. It was just past the end of Ms. Gail's shift, but she decided to take a seat across from Creionna in the cafeteria, which smelled of disinfectant and was chilly from the air conditioning.

Something about Ms. Gail's voice, a kindness foreign to Creionna, put her at ease, and she talked about her father and her fear that he would take Dominic from her. Creionna carried into that dining room the constant barrage of discouragement she'd heard from her family, the cousins and the aunts who told her she would be working at McDonald's for the rest of her life. Ms. Gail knew that for some homeless kids, that litany of doomsaying, repeated often enough, lodges in their minds, a forceful voodoo that keeps them from trying to reach their dreams. She gave Creionna a simple piece of advice: prove those voices wrong.

"Don't be embarrassed. You've come a long way," she said, giving Creionna a napkin for her eyes. "Don't be sad. You're doing good."

But first, Creionna needed a good night's sleep and some peace. Ms. Gail made sure to check in on Creionna the next day, watching her settle in, slowly making friends in the dining room, selecting some fresh clothes from the donation room, and adjusting to life in the shelter. Ms. Gail couldn't help but be impressed by the teen's determination. Not many teenagers, especially those without a permanent address, spend their time searching the Internet for the best deals on life insurance, but Creionna wanted to make extra sure that Dominic would be taken care of. And she wanted only on-the-books jobs that would provide Social Security benefits for him, if necessary.

Ms. Gail had worked at the shelter as many years as Creionna had been alive, and she knew that many new kids become paralyzed by feeling so alone in the world. They either can't or won't set goals for themselves, because they sense that the future is unlikely or pointless. Ms. Gail tries to counter that with old-fashioned, tender love and care, doled out with each serving of red beans and rice.

She was startled at how quickly Creionna rallied. Two days after Creionna entered the shelter, she had a job interview, though she found it hard to find work as a minor without a state-issued identification card. In Louisiana, minors without identification need their guardians to accompany them to obtain their official documents, but Creionna's legal guardian, Tasha, was bedridden. To get ID and find work, Creionna needed to become emancipated from the guardianship arrangement. Other minors at Covenant House face similar hurdles if they are orphaned or estranged from their parents or guardians. Cutting through the bureaucracy required many phone calls to Legal Aid lawyers, but Creionna prevailed, six months after arriving at the shelter, three months before she turned eighteen.

She started attending job training seminars and money management and parenting classes at the shelter, while Dominic played in Covenant House's free day-care center. Creionna came to work there herself, receiving a small stipend. She began to realize that her first impression about the place—"that's for dirty kids"—had been wrong.

Ms. Gail was glad to learn Creionna especially liked her meatloaf and her weekly barbecue chicken. Ms. Gail ran her kitchen to soothe the kids, to remind them that somebody loves them. She came to see the kids as family, something that was always enormously important to her. One of ten children but without children of her own, Ms. Gail takes care of her younger sister, who has Down's syndrome and lives with her. Over the years, she has grown very attached to Covenant House's young people, a bond that was sealed during Hurricane Katrina. Even though her own house stayed dry, Ms. Gail fled to Covenant House Houston, 350 miles to the west, with the kids who had holed up in the New Orleans shelter during the storm. She stayed with them for six weeks, cooking three meals a day and teaching them kitchen basics, until they all could return to New Orleans.

Even with Ms. Gail's encouragement, Creionna found it difficult to adjust to motherhood and life on her own. She had panic attacks and sharp chest pains, which sometimes coincided with Dominic's crying fits. As his bawling grew louder, she became tense and tearful. It wore her down and plunged her into bouts of despair. She did not know it at the time, but she wasn't alone. Infant crying and the parental fatigue it causes often contribute to postpartum stress and depression and can lead to shaken baby syndrome (a leading cause of child abuse deaths) and sudden infant death syndrome (SIDS), which can occur when exhausted parents put fussy babies on their stomachs to help them sleep.

But not Creionna. The shelter staff marveled at how patiently and protectively she worked with Dominic, settling him gently to sleep despite her exhaustion.

Creionna pored through *What to Expect the First Year*, which she found extremely helpful, and she came to understand how to respond when Dominic was crying, reasons why he might be fussy, and how he was supposed to sleep (on his back, to help prevent SIDS). She and the other mothers learned how to care for their babies and what toys were appropriate for different ages.

Throughout, she never let anyone else hold Dominic, although her peers often passed their babies around from counselors to other residents. She held him tight. She kept Dominic away from her own father for the first three months at Covenant House and later let her father take the baby overnight only after he signed a contract that one of her counselors helped her write. It stated that if her father did not return the baby by the designated time the next day, Creionna would call the police. At first, her father thought she was playing around, she said, but he soon realized she was completely serious, and he agreed.

Gradually, Creionna refined her future plans. She went back to high school, to finish the two classes she needed to graduate. The New Orleans schools had not served her well—her score on the ACT college entrance exam ranked her in the twenty-sixth percentile nationally. But in twelfth grade, she devoted herself to studying while Dominic slept, and she earned an A in her fine arts survey class and a B in English 4.

Feeling embarrassed by living at a homeless shelter, she wanted to enter Covenant House's Rights of Passage apartments as soon as possible. She approached Ebony Baker, the head of that program, a woman with a reggae feel and a hands-on-her-hip confidence, who explained that Creionna would have to be at least eighteen to qualify. It was the first time the two had met, and Creionna did not like Ms. Ebony's answer, or Ms. Ebony, for that matter.

Creionna kept arguing her case, and she eventually wore Ms. Ebony down. Before too long, she moved a few blocks away into one of the Rights of Passage apartments. On her new street "second line" parades, spontaneous musical celebrations that Creionna loved, broke out regularly. Dominic was crawling from wall to wall of the new apartment, which she decorated as if preparing for a flood: nothing so low to the ground that he could reach it.

Just as she began to settle into her new life, Rashad resurfaced. In January 2008, when Dominic was just thinking about starting to walk, Rashad followed Creionna one night when she was heading home and shoved her up against a wall. When she attempted to call for help, he threw down her phone, breaking it apart. He reached down into the stroller, grabbed the baby, and started running away with him. Creionna took after him, screaming. She called the police, but when they arrived, they asked her what she had done to start the fight. Once Dominic was back in her arms, she resolved to ensure that nothing similar happened again. She immediately went to court and obtained an order of protection to keep Rashad away from her.

Creionna talked to Ms. Ebony about such troubles and found her counselor, whom she was slowly growing to like, to be helpful, especially Ms. Ebony's views on the power of women. "You're special," Ms. Ebony told her. "Guys are going to do what you let them do." Creionna felt stronger in Ms. Ebony's company and began to adopt that mind-set as her own. Soon, she came to see Ms. Ebony as one of her main inspirations, along with the plays and movies of Tyler Perry, who wrote about lives of people Creionna found familiar and compelling.

As Creionna approached her eighteenth birthday in March, she noticed that she wasn't sleeping particularly well. She tossed and turned in her bed many nights, worrying that Dominic would be left without a mother. These worries, compounded by the typical sleeplessness that Dominic brought, only left her more stressed and exhausted from juggling her obligations: work, school, and, most important, raising Dominic, who was toddling around now and able to get into limitless mischief. One morning, while preparing for school, she was rushing around without a chance to think and felt a horrible pain in her chest. She sought advice from Ms. Ebony, who told her she was doing too much and never took any time for herself. "You can't help Dominic if you're not taking care of Creionna. Child, you need to leave everything in God's hands," Ms. Ebony said.

Creionna didn't welcome that last bit of advice. She hated God. Where had He been all of these years?

Ms. Gail figured she'd never met a young person with bigger plans or a longer to-do list. Yet she knew that none of it was going to happen unless Creionna cleared her heart of the anger at those who had hurt her. Creionna had to feel good about herself and believe in herself to move ahead. She reassured Ms. Gail that she was fine, but the older woman didn't believe her. One morning, Ms. Gail called her on it.

Creionna sat across from Ms. Gail after all of the kids had left the dining room. Over her half-eaten breakfast, Creionna announced that she needed a second job, to make a better living for her and Dominic. Ms. Gail wanted to be sure Creionna understood that proving to her relatives that she could support her son just was not enough. She had to make a life first, before worrying about what her family thought. She wouldn't make progress if she let them get her down. Creionna took it in and said nothing.

"You need to believe in yourself," Ms. Gail said. "You worried about what these people think of you?" Ms. Gail withdrew a small makeup mirror from her apron and showed it to Creionna, who was holding Dominic. "These are the only two people you need to worry about. What do they think of you, and that's all of it."

Inspired by some of Tyler Perry's characters, Creionna had tentatively started frequenting the nearby Shrine of St. Jude, but only when Father Anthony Rigoli was preaching, because the other priests were "too fire and brimstone" for her tastes. She searched for some sign that God cared about her, that she was wanted and loved, but she felt nothing. Her mind often drifted to bitter memories of her mother's absence, her disappointments at the hand of her father, Tasha's cruelty, Rashad's abandonment. Where was God in any of this? She often left the church aggravated.

Ms. Gail saw Creionna and Dominic in the kitchen one morning after services and greeted them warmly. "Did God bless you this morning?" she asked.

"We aren't talking," Creionna sassed. "He don't like me, and I don't like Him."

Ms. Gail said that God liked her alright. Creionna questioned where He had been lately and why He had stuck her with those crazy people in her family.

Ms. Gail looked at her for a long moment. Creionna appeared exhausted as she held Dominic on her right hip, but Ms. Gail knew he was his mother's greatest motivator. Ms. Gail never heard Creionna talk of anyone so much, and she could count on one hand the number of days that year Creionna didn't share a funny Dominic story, of his making a funny face, learning to crawl, saying his first word, or giggling incessantly.

"How you going to look at that baby and not see God on your side?" Ms. Gail laughed and gave Creionna a hug to banish the morning's blues.

One Sunday, Father Tony's sermon about letting go of anger seemed to be aimed directly at Creionna. She sat there, overwhelmed by the demands of her life as a grown-up, and realized that all of the resentment she harbored toward her grandmother wasn't helping anyone. She hated Tasha with all her heart, but the hate consumed her, distracting her at times from the joy of Dominic's forays into learning to walk or the responsibilities of work and school. She knew she had to forgive her grandmother in order to move forward, and in time, she could, freeing herself from the pain and anger that fueled so many sleepless nights.

As she turned eighteen, Creionna tackled another problem, one that had ruined her opinion of herself during her childhood. With Ms. Ebony's help, she went to a dental clinic that treats homeless people. It was the first time she had seen a dentist since breaking her tooth in a fall in second grade. She had grown accustomed to the pain in her mouth over the years and to the cramped expression she wore in every photograph. She didn't like to smile and felt nervous and embarrassed at the dental office. The dentist had to pull the broken tooth because it was infected, but soon she had a replacement. After more than a decade, it was safe to smile, she thought. And she was finding reasons to.

In February, she received an acceptance letter from Southern University, Shreveport, which included financial aid. She was heading from homelessness to higher education in eight months. Slowly, and for the first time, she started to feel hopeful about the future.

"I guess when I had people that believed in me, that supported me, that wanted to see me move on, I guess that's when it started," she said. "I consider the Covenant House workers my family. I mean, this was the first time I ever had people that believed in me and cared so deeply."

They took that job seriously. With Creionna's high school graduation nearing, some of the staff—Don Bradley, Cynthia Foots, Vantrelle Payton, among others—joined efforts to make sure she could go to her prom. They teamed up to make it all she wanted it to be.

"Proms are something that only happens once," said Mr. Don, the manager of the shelter's floor for girls. "From where she came from, she deserved to look like the queen that she is." He and others chipped in on prom arrangements, even though none of them made big salaries. They set Creionna up with a dress, shoes, and jewelry through a friend who runs a consignment boutique. Creionna chose an elegant lavender dress with crisscross straps and silver shoes that killed her feet. Ms. Foots arranged for her to have her hair and makeup done by a pro bono stylist. Creionna told him she wanted to look like a princess, and after four hours at the Master Salon, she did. The stylist fixed her hair in a high ponytail, with curls hanging down on the sides, and a tiara to finish the regal effect. When Creionna looked in the mirror, she saw a beautiful young lady—a cheerful face with a deep kindness to it and, suddenly, a new glamour. She could hardly believe how lovely she looked, and she started crying.

Creionna found it thrilling to see her classmates all dressed up. They went to a reggae club off Bourbon Street afterward, then she slipped home to be with Dominic, rather than stay overnight at the hotel room her high school girlfriends had rented. She wanted to be with her baby.

Soon afterward, she graduated, with Dominic in her arms for part of the ceremony and Covenant House staff members cheering her on. An anonymous donor helped her cover the fees for a year-book, cap and gown, and other end-of-the-year treats. She bought her own school ring and felt fulfilled by earning her diploma, something few people in her family had done.

Her friends at the predominantly black school asked Creionna about two Covenant House women who had come backstage to see her before the ceremony: "Who're those people, your parole officer?"

"No, my family," Creionna replied.

"You know, they're white," one friend cracked.

"Blood couldn't make us any thicker," Creionna said, smiling.

By mid-June, as Creionna neared the end of her time at Rights of Passage, she had become skilled at budgeting and started to see the fruits of her frugality. From her part-time job at a clinic affiliated with Tulane University, she earned $670 a month, and she paid $152 in rent, $50 in food, and $40 in gas for the car she had bought from a cousin for $1,500. After paying $60 in other expenses, she could save $300. A note on the bottom of one budget in her file reads, "Creionna has $68 of money in her pocket to spend any way she wants!!" A big smile swoops under the two dots of the exclamation points.

Despite her progress, Creionna could see a fresh batch of challenges heading her way. She had lived safely, under structured rules, in the Rights of Passage apartment with Covenant House staff supporting her, walking to work and to Dominic's day-care center. Next, she had to find a place to live in a storm-battered city, with ten thousand people ahead of her on the list for public housing. In a recession, as a single teen mom without a college degree, Creionna needed more than the sixty-eight dollars in her pocket to gain a firm footing and permanent housing.

Two years after she first walked into the New Orleans crisis shelter with her infant son, Creionna was going to college and had been promoted to be a case manager at the clinic. She was busy and spending far too many hours on the city's public transportation system. Her car had been rear-ended, and she had not been able to afford car insurance or the repairs, so she was back on the buses.

Creionna's new neighborhood, New Orleans East, had ninety-six thousand residents before Katrina and only about two-thirds as many five years later, served by just one grocery store and no hospitals—there had been two prior to the hurricane. Boarded-up houses stand among vacant grassy lots and signs that say "Coming Back Soon" and "We Cash Checks."

Creionna does not expect to live here long. Her promotion raised her salary of $15,500 a year to $22,000. Soon she will be earning too much to qualify for her hard-won Section 8 federal housing voucher that Covenant House helped her get—it pays $250 of her $645 rent.

Now, because she works for a health clinic affiliated with Tulane, she is able to take courses at the university for free. She refuses to stop going to school again—she did once, after her hectic schedule tired out Dominic so much that he started acting out at day care. She also hopes to find a safer place to live. Young men hang out in the open-air hallways of her two-story brick apartment complex, and she pointed out a broken window with dried blood on it from a not terribly recent fight. At dusk, the lights over the doors and stairs stay dark.

Her pace seems out of place here. She walks confidently in her scrubs, looking a bit taller than her five-foot frame. She wears blue eye shadow and red-auburn streaks in her hair, which is cut in a bob that turns under in a big curl. Her expression is open and friendly when she is at work, but in her apartment complex she must wear a serious game face.

Her living room light is broken, and she has to walk to the kitchen to turn on a switch that works. But she doesn't have to worry about tripping over furniture in the dark living room. There isn't any—just laundry and a carbon monoxide monitor, which chirps periodically because the battery is low.

The rest of her furniture amounts to two beds, a small flat-screen TV on the gray carpet, and a laptop. On one wall she has taped a picture of a flower in a pot, drawn by Dominic. A stuffed dog sits near his pillow in his bedroom; otherwise, that's pretty empty, too. But it's home, and it's all hers.

Dominic is smart and at three already knows how to spell his first and middle names. She corrects him when he says "Yeah" instead of "Yes" and is a little miffed that his first word was "*Dada,* the person who wasn't there for him." Usually irrepressible, he can go into a full-body pout if she gives him a time-out for showing off or if she scolds him for climbing on a tall railing. He is known around Covenant House and the clinic for saying "Yes, ma'am" and "No, ma'am," but Creionna frets that his manners fall to pieces after a weekend with her father, his now doting Papaw. Occasionally, when Creionna receives a text message from her father, she'll look over at her son as if he were a celebrity, saying, "Your people are trying to reach you."

Of course, one untimely event could derail Creionna quite quickly—another child. She realizes this and has decided to make a personal sacrifice as a way to do right by Dominic and show her appreciation to God. She has decided to be celibate.

"I had a boyfriend, he was very sweet or whatever," she said, dismissively. Dominic comes first. She has taken Ms. Gail's words to heart when it comes to banishing the voices of her naysaying family. The mirror Ms. Gail had once shown her would now reflect back an optimistic, skillful young mother, working to give Dominic the strength, encouragement, and cheerleading she hadn't known until recently.

"I want him to have the advantages and be the best he can be," she said, laughing as he carefully traced his name in crayon. The warm enthusiasm in her eyes made it easy to believe that she and her young son are going to succeed, together.

Help for Young Parents

Although books can be, should be, and have been written about ways to give young people enough love and enough faith in their futures so that they will not become parents before they become adults, Covenant House's focus is on the needs of the poor, single, young mothers who arrive at the shelter doors. They show up overwhelmed by the challenges of parenting, and their children need help to have the healthiest start possible. What can be done to give these young women the skills and confidence to raise their babies in emotionally and financially secure homes, with all of the advantages they deserve?

Special care must be taken of the children of homeless young people, because the odds are against them. A study of homeless preschoolers found that more than 20 percent of them required professional help for emotional problems, but only a third of those received any help. Homeless children of all ages are four times as likely to have asthma as are kids who have homes, and they come down with twice as many ear infections. Homelessness can even, in a way, be inherited. In one study, 20 percent of currently homeless adults had been homeless at least once before turning eighteen; in a study of homeless mothers, half had been homeless as children.

Creionna found the parenting classes at the New Orleans shelter helpful, and as of late 2011, the shelter helps other young mothers by providing Head Start classes that allow enrollment year round, which is ideal for transient young parents. In other cities, Covenant House offers various forms of parenting education—the Orlando shelter uses the Nurturing Touch curriculum, including infant massage, to stimulate healthy development and a strong attachment between mother and child. The shelter in Fort Lauderdale works with the Healthy Start Coalition of Broward County, with two staff members instructing pregnant and parenting young people in proper prenatal care, breastfeeding, smoking cessation, parenting techniques, and how to take care of themselves as well. And Covenant House Alaska's transitional living program for pregnant and parenting young women, known as Passage House, teaches them to be competent nurturers and skilled leaders.

For the last thirty years, Nurse-Family Partnership has helped young and impoverished first-time mothers by providing a registered nurse to visit them in their homes from the first trimester through the child's second birthday. The nurses offer prenatal care, parenting techniques, and coaching sessions. In New York City, a team of nurses from the program serves women and teens in homeless shelters. Studies have documented the program's effectiveness in preventing child abuse and neglect, improving a child's readiness for school, and helping mothers become more self-sufficient. One analysis of the program found it saved society almost twenty-five thousand dollars per high-risk family, by increasing employment, reducing reliance on public assistance, and lowering health, education, and criminal justice–related expenses.

The promising model of the Young Family Critical Time Intervention uses the effective "housing first" approach, placing young mothers and their children from homeless shelters into stable housing, offering parenting education and mental health and substance abuse treatment to the moms, and working with them to obtain medical care and income support and, as they become more independent, to form closer ties with their families and communities. A pilot program in New York State's Westchester County has shown promise, with none of the fifty young mothers getting pregnant again in the next eighteen to twenty-four months of the program. At the time the study began, in 2000, the county had the highest per capita rate of homelessness in New York State.

Connecting mothers and infants with social services helps, of course, but keeping them connected with fathers would be priceless. It is telling and tragic that every young person in this book lacked a consistently nurturing father living with them during their childhood. Ideally, programs that encourage young fathers to be involved in the lives of their children can help establish long-lasting bonds between father and child, reduce stress on the mom, and bolster the child's chances of success in school and beyond.

Many single parents do a remarkable job raising children well, but the statistics about growing up in a single-parent family are beyond sobering. According to the Fatherhood Initiative:

- Compared to living with both parents, living in a single-parent home doubles the risk that a child will suffer physical, emotional, or educational neglect.
- Fatherless children are twice as likely to drop out of school and twice as likely to repeat a grade.
- Children in father-absent homes are five times more likely to be poor and 54 percent more likely to be poorer than their fathers.
- Teens without fathers are twice as likely to be involved in early sexual activity and seven times more likely to become pregnant as adolescents.
- A survey of seven thousand inmates revealed that 39 percent lived in mother-only households. In a study of almost fourteen thousand female inmates, more than half grew up without their fathers.

There are an estimated 7.2 million low-income fathers in the United States who do not live with their children. Many young fathers may even be reluctant to take paternity tests, for fear that they will be forced to pay child support. Too often, relationships break down between young moms and dads, with fathers facing roadblocks to visitation from the mother and her family, usually the custodial caregivers.

Those who study fatherhood programs note that when fathers have family members or friends who can support and help negotiate the relationship between father and child, the paternal bond can grow stronger. Likewise, fatherhood support groups, such as one made up of graduates from the Fathers Now program in Newark, New Jersey, can help men remind one another of the importance of staying involved in their children's lives, no matter how difficult that can be. Programs that pair experienced fathers with new ones can make all the difference, said Vivian Gadsden, the director of the National Center on Fathers and Families, especially for young fathers who grew up without strong male role models.

If such efforts can take hold and spread, fewer young people will have to find their way through childhood and adolescence without the benefit of two involved, loving role models.

Kazandra stayed in the Port Authority Bus Terminal before Covenant House. She plans to write a book about her sixteen years in foster care.

The photographs in this gallery were taken by Timothy Ivy at Covenant House in New York. Back row: Victor, Jawara, Michael. Middle row: Kevin Ryan, Christian, Vincent, Diana, Elvis. Front row: Tina Kelley, Maria, LaKheem, Stephanie.

Diana lived at Covenant House until recently and is the assistant manager at the shelter's kitchen. She considers it a challenging privilege to manage a staff of shelter residents.

Latoya works two jobs while training to become an emergency medical technician and hopes to become a nurse. She came to Covenant House after living at Green Chimneys, a shelter for LGBT kids.

Joseph left home at fifteen and couch-surfed for five years. He looked up
"homeless youth" on the Internet and found Covenant House. He wants to
start his own record label.

Vincent is a cook in the kitchen and is living in the Rights of Passage transitional living program. He's proud to have gotten a high school diploma and a steady job.

Wolph, right, who is studying grammar in the classroom with teacher Andre Ford, wants to become a police officer because he wants to protect people.

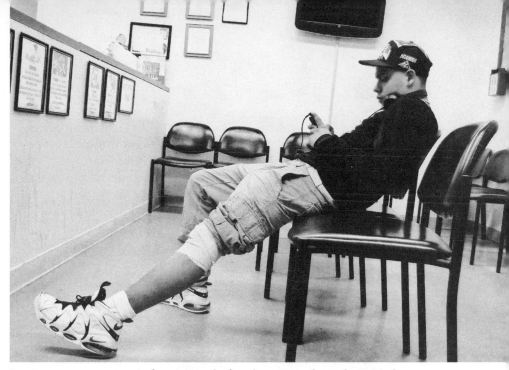

Louis spent ten years in foster care before becoming homeless. He has an apartment now, but still visits Covenant House's medical clinic.

Nyleve received her security training certification from Covenant House and comes back for health care and help finding work, which is not easy in this economy.

Angelina and her daughter, Maleah, almost three, spent two years without a stable home. They lived with friends, various family members, and at another shelter while Angelina struggled to keep her jobs.

At Covenant House, Victor wrote his first resume and got a new suit for interviews. "The trust I never had for anyone, I could bring out. Knowing me and the staff that's around me, we'll break through."

148

Matt, who lived in his car while homeless, has been accepted into drama school and has a scholarship from Covenant House.

Kevara and her daughter, Nacirema, live in Covenant House's Rights of Passage program, where Kevara is studying to earn her high school equivalency diploma. She wants to be a chef.

"I'm actually pretty good at being homeless," said Michael, who had twelve foster placements. At Covenant House he has found two jobs. "It's almost like going through a war. I can't be beat. I can't give up."

Bien-Kachylah came to New York after the 2010 Haiti earthquake. She wants to study nursing and medicine to fulfill her childhood dream of becoming a doctor.

Lamar has trained for three years to be a boxer. He had his own place in Harlem once, but couldn't afford it. "What's hard is knowing you have no one to listen to but yourself."

In 2011, Elvis ran the New York City Half Marathon, raising money for Covenant House. Running helps him relieve the stresses of being homeless.

5

A Teenager with Nowhere to Go and His Mentor

Keith's and Jim's Stories

When you think of the tiny scenes that create a childhood—talking in funny accents around the dinner table, taking long walks with the dog, practicing for big games, preparing for holidays—you unwittingly take so much for granted. Keith's mother killed his father and, several years later, left her three sons at home and never came back. What kind of childhood memories can be created out of that void? And how does Keith even begin to build a life for himself?

Three little boys, the oldest only in first grade, lived in a cramped, two-bedroom apartment in Newark, New Jersey, and their stomachs were growling. Their mother had been gone for more than a day, leaving them alone again. An alcoholic addicted to crack cocaine, she frequently vanished for days, and the boys' various fathers were long gone. Whenever she reappeared the boys became accustomed to the same routine. She rounded them up and brought them to the store, instructing them to stuff in their pants whatever the family needed, while she held the attention of the clerk at the counter. When she was gone from their apartment and the refrigerator was empty, the boys sometimes snuck out at night to find food on their own, scavenging trash, celebrating the occasional half-empty box of Cheerios they could find.

On this night in 1985, the middle brother, Keith Dawson, who was five, decided to make toast instead of pilfering the neighborhood garbage cans. The boys agreed, and they reached as high as they could to the top of the gas stove, put slices of bread directly on the burner, and turned the knob to ignite the flame.

Within a minute, plumes of black smoke billowed up, some venting through a partially opened window. Confused, the boys stared at the fire, watching smoke fill the room, paint the walls with splashes of black, and fill the air with a heaviness that suddenly made it difficult to breathe.

They froze. This wasn't supposed to happen. They had seen adults make toast; hadn't the grown-ups placed the bread directly on the stove? The smoke triggered an alarm in the apartment building that pierced the air, but the throbbing refrain in Keith's head was louder: *"Mama's gonna be so mad when she gets back."*

She was not to be messed with. Ever. Two years earlier, Keith had overheard his parents having a terrifying fight, and afterward he never saw his father again. Keith would learn years later that his mother had allegedly killed his father by smashing a couple of bottles against his head. She never went to jail, and the boys, who were home but too young to recall the scene, did not learn of her role in his death until adolescence. They were just happy that the fighting between the grown-ups had stopped.

The parents' shouting matches had often lasted long into the night. Keith pulled a pillow over his ears whenever their hollering went past his bedtime. He could not have known how his mother's crack habit fueled the rage. While his older brother, Keiran, somehow managed to drift off to sleep in the room they shared, Keith often tossed and turned well past midnight. Doctors attributed his restlessness and insomnia to extensive prenatal crack exposure. During nights of the loudest brawls between his parents, he wriggled and writhed just a bit less than he had as a newborn crack baby.

Chaos reigned in their low-rent, rundown apartment. Their young mother allowed men in and out of her apartment, too stoned on most days to notice how visitors treated her boys. She took up with a parade of drug dealers whose penchant for violence worsened over time. One of them barged into the apartment one afternoon. Keith had no idea what was going on, but the man kept asking the boys' mother where the money was, yelling that she'd better have it. He swung toward her, while she begged him to leave. Keith, all of four years old, lunged at the intruder and bit his leg. In one sweeping gesture, the man lifted Keith and smashed his small frame against the wall, busting his skull and dislocating several bones.

Now, as smoke filled the kitchen from the burning toast, Keith's mind raced. He was afraid of the fire, the smoke, and his mama. As the black cloud crept slowly downward toward the boys, Keith closed his arms around Keiran and his younger brother, Burton, who was only two, and they crouched low for better air.

Across the Hudson River a decade earlier, Jim White seethed at his father from the St. Francis Prep football field. The starting quarterback for his high school junior varsity team, Jim had taken a huge hit in the corner, tumbling backward for a major loss of yards. The boys' coach fumed from the sidelines, but the team was transfixed on another sight: Jim White Sr. leaping from the stands, his hands raised, yelling about his son's hit. He raced onto the field, bellowing at the coaches. Jim, sixteen, had been piqued by his father's erratic outbursts of late, but now, he was mortified.

Raised in Flushing, Queens, Jim was part of a close, church-going family, with high standards for behavior that kept everyone in line. His mother bore six children in seven years, including "Irish twins," as she liked to say: two children born eleven months apart but in the same year: Liz in January and Jim in December. Both parents were devout Roman Catholics, and the family filled an entire pew each week on the right side of Mary's Nativity Church in front of the pieta. The children excelled in sports, theater, and school, and from a distance, they appeared to be the all-American family.

Yet that impression masked the Whites' growing anxiety that something terrible was happening to their father and to them. Once a silver-tongued pharmaceuticals salesman who charmed clients, friends, and family with ease, he had gradually become unpredictable and insular. He got lost, ran late, forgot important family commitments, was prone to eruptions, and struggled at work. The loving banter he and his wife, Mary, had shared for twenty years was shattered at times by his angry, frustrated flare-ups. The children recoiled. This was not the gentle, quick-to-laugh father they had known; that man was slipping away. A whistleblower at work finally reported him for neglecting his clients and using drugs or alcohol, and Mr. White was reprimanded and demoted.

Jim's mother felt certain that something else was going on, and she was consumed with getting to the bottom of her husband's behavior. She led him to doctors, specialists, psychotherapists, psychiatrists, New Age herbalists, and even an exorcist. Nothing worked. Each small joy the family had shared with Jim Sr. drifted away, one by one.

Even tennis, a game that bonded Jim and his father more than any other, became a drag. Jim, accepted to Mercy College in nearby Westchester County on a tennis scholarship, loved playing with his father, but the man's gait changed, then his serve slacked, and eventually he was given to odd, twisting movements that made matches unbearable. Jim eagerly fled to college.

Soon afterward, doctors solved the cause of his father's decline: Huntington's disease, a hereditary neurodegenerative disorder that affects muscle coordination and leads to cognitive decline and dementia. A wave of dread and relief washed over the Whites. Here at last was an explanation, a vindication from the rumors that had swirled. And yet the cause of their father's decade-long descent turned out to be a vicious disease that would claim his mind and body before taking his life.

Jim was struck by remorse, a guilt that sat darkly in his heart. He dwelled on the stages and spaces of life when he had shrunk away from his father and winced at his odd behavior. Others felt the same way—when the Whites attended a friend's retirement party, the host spoke endearingly of Jim's father to the packed room and announced to many the news of his diagnosis. After the speech and a great ovation, a man in a business suit approached Mary and her children, his face pale and awash in tears. He knelt before her, a scene the children cannot forget to this day, and begged her pardon.

"I'm the one who reported your husband at work for abusing drugs and alcohol," he confessed. "It was me." Broken by the weight of the news that a disease, not substance abuse, had caused the problems, he whispered through tears, "I am so sorry. Please, please forgive me."

Mary, stoic and never one for public scenes, took the man's hand and encouraged him to his feet. "My husband has already forgiven you," she smiled.

The words floored Jim. He needed that forgiveness, too, from his father perhaps, but more so from himself. He couldn't shake the sense that he had betrayed his father each time he had been embarrassed by him, on the football field, on the tennis court, in the neighborhood. It ate him up.

The door to Keith's apartment burst open, pulling smoke into the hallway, and a squad of firemen passed by the boys, quickly extinguished the fire, and left the place rancid with smoke.

The firemen asked the boys where their parents were. They had no idea. The big men in dirty jackets and monster masks terrified Keith, and he wanted his mama to tell them to go away. He wanted her so badly then.

Child protection workers eventually brought Keith and Keiran to Melina Dawson, a single mother and an experienced foster parent, nearly fifty, who lived in a modest home in nearby Irvington; Burton, just a toddler, was placed with another foster family. In those first nights with Miss Dawson, Keith's insomnia persisted, and he fretted about his mama. How would she ever find him?

Days became weeks, then months, but Keith's mother did not emerge to reclaim her sons. The more time that lapsed, the less clearly he remembered her face, which made him anxious. All he could recall was her back, dark and bony, just as it appeared to him one night long ago after the intruder had slammed him against the wall. Keith replayed that night over and over again. He was lying in the tub as the faucet was running, and he felt paralyzed by his injuries. His mother was on the phone with her back to him, and the tub was quickly filling. Keith started slipping down and couldn't stop himself. He was so scared, but he could not call out to her. The water reached his top teeth before she turned around and noticed.

During grade school, living with Miss Dawson, Keith had a recurring daydream. *I will go outside and my mother will be there, and she'll be like, "I was just playing, come on, we can go home now."* The fantasy transfixed him. If his mother returned, they could be a family again, with Burton coming back to his brothers, where he belonged. As the bad memories of the hardships she put them through faded, so did vivid recollections of her features. Keith was haunted by the blur of her face.

Miss Dawson sensed more than Keith's pining for his mother. She felt his resistance to her, his unwillingness to trust her or accept that her house was his home. He refused to hug her or show affection of any kind. Loving her somehow meant giving up on his mother's return. Miss Dawson ached when she saw his pain and his surliness.

There might be one way to ease his heartache, she thought. Maybe reuniting the brothers would help them all move forward. So, after nearly three years, she offered to raise Burton as well. Faith and family mattered enormously to her; they were the center of her life, and she hoped to share them with the boys. Burton's return marked the happiest day of their young lives. Keith was grateful, marveling at how Miss Dawson had put them back together again. Not long after that, she adopted all three of them, and they came to call her Mawson, for Mother Dawson. The adoption saved them from the pinball nightmares of long-term foster care, where children can bounce from one home to another in a long, bumpy decline.

Keith was nine when he officially became Mawson's adoptive son, but it was not the new beginning some heralded for him. He still felt a nagging misery, missing his birth mother and believing that his new mother could not ever quite take her place. Despite Mawson's best efforts, he still resented her.

Mawson, who wears her graying hair high and tidy, was a firm, frugal parent. She was not one for frills such as fast food or brand names. A daughter of the poor, segregated South, where survival meant keeping one's head low and living within one's means, she reminded the boys that she and her ten siblings had grown up fine without hundred-dollar sneakers in rural North Carolina. The boys came to think of her as straight-up and old school. She felt determined to raise them as young men of Christ and character. Every morning, before the boys headed off to school, she and her sons joined hands and read a Bible verse. "I've always had God there to direct me," she told them. "No matter what you do out there, when you come in here, this is what we do in here."

They had reason to pray—for healing for the boys; for financial security to make ends meet on Mawson's salary at an insurance company, where she was the only black person in her office; and for safety as they went about their lives in Irvington, a poor, forgotten stepchild of a township just west of Newark. Keith grew up four blocks from the lowest-ranked high school in New Jersey, on a street where drug dealers ruled the sidewalks, and everyone else stayed inside. Until 1965, Irvington was almost entirely white, but after the Newark riots of 1967, many African Americans moved one town west, to Irvington, which is now 85 percent black. In 2004, seven teenagers were killed in street violence before the end of the summer. In 2011, it ranked as the eighth most violent city in the United States.

Keith was always good in math, but school did not inspire him. He was antsy and introverted, and he stayed up late, stoked by the restlessness from his earliest years. He spent most of middle school in special education classes and wore thick black glasses that the kids mocked. Although his friends were few and far between, he watched the other children—indeed, everything around him—with great interest. He was a child who paid attention, who listened intently, and who was always thinking. Sometimes he just sat in the grass and looked at the sky, the clouds, the trees, how God put all of that together, made every leaf perfect, and it simply amazed him.

The older Keith got, the more Mawson enjoyed his thoughtfulness. He was more exciting than any of her other children. He engaged with her, speaking his mind and asking questions. He gradually came to see her as not only a good foster parent, but a good mother, a counselor, a nurturer who knew how to bring certain things out of him. As he grew older and more handsome, Keith also came to care more about how he looked, and Mawson encouraged him at every turn. But she believed he needed a man to help him navigate his teen years and relied on her brother, who lived with her to teach Keith and his brothers how to be men. The boys and their uncle shared their feelings about faith and church, girls, school, and the streets. The minute the boys "started smelling themselves," as Mawson put it, she felt them leaving her arms to join the hustle of life beyond her home. Before long, Keith had graduated from high school and was on his way to college.

"Be careful," Mawson told him. "There is no going backwards once you're out there."

It was a wise warning.

After Mercy College, Jim decided to volunteer full time at Covenant House in Manhattan as a member of the Faith Community, a faith-based Peace Corps of sorts, where recent college graduates and people from various professions devote a year to work with homeless kids and reside with other volunteers in a community house. The program combines traditional Roman Catholic–inspired service to the poor with prayer and meditation. It was a surprising choice for Jim, whose friends had embraced the opportunities of corporate America, with a privileged few claiming positions as young traders on Wall Street. Jim had been the center of the universe at St. Francis Prep and at Mercy College, a star athlete, a talented student, a popular leader. Why had he broken ranks to slog away at a homeless shelter in one of the most rundown parts of Hell's Kitchen? He wasn't quite sure, and it made him twitchy.

A handsome guy's guy with dark hair, an offbeat and off-color sense of humor, and a magnetic personality, Jim was a favorite among his fellow volunteers, cracking up his colleagues with raucous reenactments of the day's events. Yet the clown in him cavorted several layers above a deep and thoughtful spirituality, a yearning for the presence of God in his life. A reader and writer of poetry, Jim wove poems into the conversation, uplifting simple exchanges with pitch-perfect recitations. The Faith Community afforded him daily opportunities for all of this—prayer, poetry, and reflection—and forced him to confront the hard questions he had skirted since his father's diagnosis: was he searching for something or running from something?

Turns out, it was a little of both. After months of careful reflection, Jim recognized he had come to Covenant House to help kids but also, in part, to escape the pain of his father's deterioration. His compass then pointed in one steady direction: homeward. He simply had to seek his father's forgiveness. Although his mother reassured him repeatedly that his father loved him, Jim wanted his father to know how strongly he loved him right back.

"Sometimes we run and we run, and only home can make us whole," Jim said to a friend in the Faith Community, echoing the yearnings of many of the kids he had counseled at the shelter. "We have to turn back and make peace in order to move forward." That year, one of Jim's favorite poets, David Whyte, published *Songs for Coming Home*, in which he wrote:

> It is the opening of eyes long closed.
> It is the vision of far off things
> seen for the silence they hold.
> It is the heart after years
> of secret conversing
> speaking out loud in the clear air.

Jim's heart led him the length of the number 7 subway train, from Times Square back to Flushing. He went home to his father, who by then was spending most of his time in a rented hospital bed in the family's living room. Mary had devoted herself fully to caring for her husband, preserving their home life for as long as possible, bathing, feeding, and changing him. As the disease gradually stole his ability to speak, the couple began learning a new language, a Huntington's argot all their own, which Mary interpreted to the world.

Jim sat at his father's bedside and looked into his eyes, beginning to cry. "I'm sorry, Dad," he said.

But Jim Sr. would have none of it. Cautiously, his father labored a response, "You're doing God's work, Jimmy." Jim bowed his head, hoping to conceal the tears.

Straining to clasp Jim's hand, his father reached over to him and with great effort met his eyes squarely: "I am proud of you, son."

The words buoyed Jim, propelling him forward to the work of his heart, work his ailing father so admired.

After two years of serving kids as a volunteer, Jim joined the shelter's staff and devoted himself to the agency's most important new project: designing, building, and running a transitional housing program for homeless youth who were moving from the shelter to independence. Covenant House was expanding, and its work now had to include programs that helped kids move off the streets sustainably, giving them choices beyond gangs, drugs, and violence. The program would be called Rights of Passage, spelled that way because all kids, no matter their circumstances, have the right to be loved, the right to be housed, and the right to make a supported, dignified passage into adulthood.

Building Rights of Passage was a deeply satisfying experience for Jim, and once the kinks of the start-up had been resolved, he set his sights on what was next for him. In 1986, he was recruited by Covenant House donors to work at Bear Stearns, the large financial services firm, and he decided to join their new training program and give Wall Street a whirl. He traded Treasury bills on the famously hectic and high-octane trading floor, and his salary skyrocketed. The energy and locker-room bawdiness of the floor exhilarated him at first, but it wore off in time, and he missed Covenant House, especially the kids. He figured he'd earn a lot of money, then go back to helping Covenant House through philanthropy, after an early retirement.

Three years later, when Jim was twenty-nine, his sister, Liz, fell ill with Huntington's disease, even as it was slowly killing her father. Liz, a sweet-natured, married mother of two, became sicker faster than her father had. On some level, the family had understood the risks for all of them when their father was diagnosed. The disease is caused by a genetic mutation, and each of the siblings had a 50 percent risk of it. Yet Liz's diagnosis and deterioration sent shock waves through them. Within months, Mary was straining to nurse her husband and her daughter, while mothering Liz's children and raising money among family and friends to fund research for a cure. Jim watched helplessly as the disease ransacked his family, destroying his father and rapidly robbing his sister of her vitality. Grieving, he wondered who among them would be next.

Liz's decline forced Jim to reckon with the future. Pushing thirty and earning a six-figure salary but feeling unfulfilled at Bear Stearns, he longed for more meaningful work. He sometimes awoke on Sundays in a sweat, dreading his return Monday to the trading floor. Unsure whether he also carried Huntington's time bomb, he abruptly quit the firm, sold his car and his apartment, and returned home to discern his next steps.

It didn't take him long to decide to go back to Covenant House in 1990, even though many were leaving it at the time. Its founder, Father Bruce Ritter, had recently stepped down amid allegations of financial improprieties and having inappropriate relationships with homeless young people in his care.

Jim and the people then working on the front lines at Covenant House were crushed. Thousands of volunteers and staff members had felt deeply proud to help desperate kids, but news of Father Ritter's behavior shattered many, causing them to quit. Many former supporters of the charity were embarrassed and disillusioned. Yet Jim believed in the mission and hoped the arrival of the charity's new president, Sister Mary Rose McGeady, a sixty-three-year-old, tough-as-nails veteran of Catholic Charities, would signal a new beginning for Covenant House.

In 1994, she asked Jim to establish Covenant House's newest shelter, in Newark, New Jersey. It was a tall order in a city that, in those days, had an unfriendly administration, but Jim, who had moved to New Jersey, jumped at the opportunity. He was fond of encouraging the staff with a piece of advice from his Catholic upbringing, "Preach the Gospel always, every day, every minute, every second. And if you have to, use words." He wanted his Covenant House team to be role models of absolute respect and unconditional love, cornerstones of the mission, and he knew that few of the kids in the shelter had ever received the most basic pep talk from family, friends, or teachers. The staff members at Covenant House in Newark had to become those voices.

He brought them together in those first days and urged them to see each of the kids as extraordinary but in need of rewiring. "Often, the kids define themselves as a foster kid," he said. "But that's not who they are. When you're in the system, you churn out your resume of abuse and neglect. In those moments we have to try to rephrase that.

"If I have a patron saint," Jim urged, "it has to be Veronica at Calvary. Does she grab the back of the cross as Christ passes? No. Does she wail and lament his crucifixion? No. Is she standing in outrage, chastising the soldiers? No, no, no."

Then Jim lowered his voice, almost to a whisper, "She kneels before him and wipes his brow. She is just *there*. Quietly, with genuine love, *there*. Sometimes that's what Covenant House is. It's like the words my father once said to me in his hospital bed. What did he say? 'Proud of you, son.' That's it. If you're going to work with our kids for any length of time, you have to know this." He held up as an example the caseworker who made sure to offer each newcomer a cup of tea during the intake interview, to help the young person feel special and more at home.

While Jim was helping the Newark shelter team plan its move into a spacious, renovated warehouse on Washington Street in the city's Central Ward, just a few blocks from City Hall, he harbored grave doubts about what was in store for him. Having watched his father deteriorate and die and Lizzy suffer, he couldn't help but worry for his sisters, Winnie, Mary, and Eileen, and his brother,

Tommy. He wondered if he had passed along the Huntington's gene to his own children and whether the disease would ultimately call his name. A medical test can determine whether one carries the genetic mutation that causes Huntington's, but most of Jim's siblings had decided not to be tested. Jim swayed back and forth, at times leaning hard against it, and at other times inclined. He knew he just had to decide, or the disease might reveal itself before he chose.

Keith headed off to Rutgers University to study engineering and fiber optics, but he found that he could not understand the computer language Fortran to save his life. He struggled mightily in his classes, feeling unprepared by his high school, which had offered no computer courses. He lasted a year before his financial aid was rescinded. He joined the navy and worked a short stint as an aviation electronics technician in Florida. It didn't suit him, and he was discharged for fighting with a sailor who called him a racial epithet. From there, he went to the Job Corps but got kicked out for drinking when he was nineteen. It was an ominous first warning that the alcohol and later the drugs that had consumed his birth mother would also keep him from navigating his own life, even while they helped him forget the disasters of his childhood.

Mawson cared deeply for Keith and worried about him when one effort after another collapsed. She had kept her home open to her grown children, even as she continued to care for young foster children, and Keith returned to live with her from time to time. Yet she was badly shaken to discover that one of the other young people in her home had brought cocaine and marijuana into her house. She had young children to protect, and she made clear that none of the older boys, including Keith, could stay with them if he was smoking pot, drinking, and coming home long after midnight.

By then, addiction began to grip Keith—alcohol and marijuana, mostly. He wasn't about to let go of either, and he made his choice, spending about a month living on the streets of Newark, in abandoned buildings or cars. In the middle of winter, desperately cold, he tried Newark's Fulton Street shelter for single adults. Exhausted from roaming the streets for days, he nearly collapsed into the cot. The men were much older, and he did not feel safe staying in a room with thirty of them. He caught a few hours' sleep with his boots in his arms, but he left early the next morning.

Arriving at Covenant House

Keith turned as a last resort to the Covenant House in Newark, a city that has worked hard to bounce back from the race riots of 1967. More than three decades later, economic opportunities had remained limited. In 2000, soon after Keith arrived at the shelter, only 48 percent of Newark's high school students graduated in five years, and more than 37 percent of its children lived below the poverty line.

In his first days at Covenant House, Keith tried to hide a deepening drug habit, bending the truth about his fatigue and his lateness, manipulating staff members with his 500-watt smile and pliant personality. In fact, he was paying almost no attention to anyone. All of Keith's false starts blended together in his head, and the drugs and the booze lulled him just enough to quiet the noise. In many respects, his approach was typical among kids who have lived on the street, who have had to be savvy to survive. Many have learned to tell authority figures what they want to hear, to make it through the day. And many have followed Keith's path of wearing a constant happy face, because no one wants to be around a downer, and there's no clear way to solve a twenty-year-old stack of problems anyway.

Once in a while he told his story, and he sensed pity or judgment in the reaction, which he loathed. He felt ashamed. He tried to bottle up the panic about his dimming prospects, but for the first time in his life he was beginning to feel completely hopeless.

It took time at Covenant House, but Keith rallied, starting to attend drug counseling, working several part-time jobs, and saving money. In 2001, he was accepted back into Rutgers. The staff took great pride in his decision to return to college and threw him a party, with red balloons and a cake specially made by the cooks in the shelter kitchen.

At the beginning of the party, one of the administrators who usually worked upstairs approached him and asked who Keith was. Keith laughed and said he was Keith, and the man congratulated him.

"Anything you need, just call me," the man said.

Keith could not help but think to himself, "*Who is this white dude, coming up to me, maybe trying to show off? I know you're a big shot, but what's 'anything you need'? I never met you before. How am I supposed to find your phone number? All right. Whatever.*" Keith knew that anyone extending an offer like that was not going to pick up the phone, even if Keith ever managed to call. He had been to this movie before. At best, he would get a "we'll call you," and he knew they never would. He shrugged off the man and his hint of corporate polish.

Keith did not think much about that first encounter with Jim White, but a day or so later, Jim found Keith in the shelter and asked him to have lunch around the corner at Je's, a family-owned soul food restaurant. With its menu overflowing with comfort food and its waitresses oozing grandmotherly charm, Je's was the perfect place to unwind and relax. Jim asked Keith dozens of questions, trying to get to know him and discover his interests. Jim asked about his hopes and dreams, but Keith said he really didn't have any. Jim doubted that, but knew that not everyone has the self-confidence to explore them.

They started to talk, really talk, and a second lunch followed, then a third, and before long it was routine for them to spend time together each week, catching up, talking about the future. A friendship blossomed. Jim didn't give much in the way of advice, he just took Keith and his future seriously. There was a kindness in Jim that Keith admired, and he began to rely on Jim in emergencies, once when he needed a hundred dollars to restore his driver's license after it was suspended over unpaid tickets, and once when he was robbed at gunpoint—he got hit in the head and lost three hundred dollars, all of the money to pay his bills. Jim loaned Keith the money, which Keith paid back by doing handyman work.

Over time, Jim's moral support helped Keith meet his basic survival needs and then his more advanced ones. By believing in Keith and encouraging him to believe in himself, Jim goaded him to face up to his problems and stay connected to a caring community. Jim prepared him to be ready to believe in something bigger than himself. As Keith grew more confident, Jim could support him in reaching for higher goals, such as developing future plans and building better relationships.

Keith went back to Rutgers and completed a year before he received a letter that his financial aid package had fallen through again. He had just talked with the basketball coach about the possibility of joining the team when he felt the rug pulled out from him one more time. Soon, he was back with Covenant House, deeply embarrassed.

It was a hurtful time, back to square one. He felt pressure at Covenant House to make a new plan, but he didn't have it in him. He felt he had failed at everything he tried. He balled himself up on one of the shelter's benches, hoping to sleep away the day, the week, this life. He saw both of his brothers occasionally, but he did not spend much time with them, feeling the burden of their expectations. He was dying inside, outwardly indolent and inwardly convinced he was a failure. He turned to his old friends, marijuana and alcohol, to numb the gnawing sense of disgrace that choked him. He depended on that momentary peace and disorientation, looking forward to his daily high as much as he had once looked forward to breakfast or, more boldly, college. He allowed drugs and booze to wash over him, claiming him as they had taken his mother years earlier.

Jim was distraught by Keith's breakdown. He suspected that addiction and depression were unraveling Keith, but he did not want to pounce on him and drive him away. He could see that Keith was in enormous pain and invited him to lunch several times. When Keith appeared late and stoned, Jim matter-of-factly ended their meeting, saying, "Sorry, you're high, and I am not having lunch with you in this condition." After several more encounters like that, Jim called for a "courageous conversation."

They met the next day, outside the shelter on Pearl Street, a narrow one-way drive bordering the building in Newark.

"Look, Keith, I'm telling you this because I care about you and I care where you end up in life. You need to get yourself together. You're using, I know it and you know it. You're getting high and drunk, and if . . ."

"Wait a second," Keith interrupted.

Jim stopped him cold. "No, let me finish, my man. I know you. You are a sweet talker, and I'm sure you have some sweet story to tell me. Save it. I know what's going down here, and so do you, and if you don't wake up, you're going to get stuck on these streets, or worse."

The words stung, but Keith held his tongue. He only shook his head back and forth, turned, and walked away. Jim watched Keith grow small down the street, hoping he had not pressed the throttle too hard. Keith was a cliff walker, like many of the young people at Covenant House, teetering on a ledge that separated solid ground from free fall. Jim wanted to make an impression, but he hoped his words had not tilted Keith in the wrong direction.

That night in bed, Keith, down from his midmorning high and slightly hung over, replayed Jim's words in his mind. Hours later, they still burned. He was crestfallen and wanted to hop out of bed right then and prove to Jim that he could turn things around, that Jim could be proud of him. The desire surprised Keith. He was shocked to see how much Jim's opinion of him mattered.

The next day Keith sought out Jim in the lounge.

"I messed up, Jim. Dang it," Keith said, trying to explain himself. When you don't have a mother, you don't have a father, and rotten things happen to you when you're younger, he said, it makes you feel like you have no control. What would stop more bad things from happening? Kids from successful families grow up knowing they're supposed to be lawyers or doctors, but Keith's birth family's traditions included addiction and violent death. As he spoke to Jim, the despair in his eyes was more palpable than in any of their previous encounters.

"Your past doesn't define who you're going to be," Jim said. "It's okay to look back in the rearview mirror, but don't stare. You can learn from your history, but don't let it define you."

KEITH'S THOUGHTS ON THE
MEANING OF A MENTOR

Covenant House was so intricate, it could give everyone what they needed at every level. I was missing self-confidence, accountability, things like that. Having someone see me in another light, having someone really, really believe in me, it makes you think. Jim didn't deal with me like no McDonald's job. He was speaking more "If you want to go to the height, there are certain sacrifices you've got to make." When he started challenging me, it hurt, but it felt good. I'd feel ashamed, but I'd want to prove to him I could do this. In an encouraging way, a loving way, he was very precise with that cut. It was to get that cancer out. It was, "I'm only telling you this because I care about you and I care where you end up in life."

He knew how to say it to me and let me know he was serious, but he loved me. It wasn't like he was my boss, but I looked up to him in that sense. If he said, "I didn't like how you did that," I'd feel, "Dang, I messed up."

I've gotten to a place to where I'm pursuing my dreams. He makes me feel secure, like everything's going to be all right. I've got to put 140 percent in this. It's what I do now. When I'm working, I put my all into it. The night before, I can hardly sleep, I'm thinking of any possibility that could go wrong. I have to do everything to a T.

God has blessed me to have many people who just care. I wouldn't trade my life for anybody's. I wouldn't trade what I went through for anybody. I became this from what I went through. I became compassionate because there was a time I needed compassion. I'm so caring because there was a time I wanted someone to care. I remember that feeling. Why would I want to put that on anyone else? That hurt.

Jim will tell me, "You just start doing calculated moves, calculated good moves, maybe a good move a year, and it can push you forward." It makes me do so much more. When you constantly have that in your corner, it's a blessing.

Even as he spoke those words, they boomeranged for Jim. He did not want to live his life in the shadow of Huntington's. He had vacillated long enough and decided to undergo the medical test to determine whether he carried the genetic marker.

Jim learned in a doctor's office at the University of Medicine and Dentistry of New Jersey that he did not. He still mourned his father and his sister, but he was relieved, even joyful, that his four children would not endure the suffering their grandfather and aunt had faced. His mother would not bury more Whites from this branch of her tree.

Jim was not sure Keith would fare as well, especially after Keith learned that his brother had run into their birth mother on the street. After so many years, she was barely recognizable: drunk, strung out on a corner, looking for spare change for her next hit. Keith agonized to think of her this way, the drugs still firmly in control. He remembered reading in his foster care file at Mawson's home that New Jersey's child welfare system had offered his mother a chance to take back her sons, but she decided to let them go. Maybe she knew that she was fated for this life—if that's what it was—of hopeless addiction. Keith had fantasized about her over the years, imagining that she had pulled herself together and found some happiness away from crack. Now he saw how silly those dreams had been, and he began to worry that he was on the same path, as he came to discover how firmly he had fallen into addiction. If this was his destiny, he would surrender.

Discouraged and unable to find work, Keith left Covenant House in a huff. He spent more time on the streets and tried his hand at selling drugs. It was a living, until his lack of street skills caught up with him. He got arrested across the street from Mawson's and spent almost two weeks in jail, in part because the guy he was working for didn't want to spend $310 to bail him out. It was only a misdemeanor charge but a new low for Keith. He remembers spending six or seven days in quarantine—twenty-three hours alone, an hour for exercise—while his tuberculosis tests were processed, and he hated it. He was disconsolate, tired of what he was doing and of how he was doing it.

Jim did not give up on him and encouraged him to accept work at a hundred dollars a week with a neighborhood barber, who lent Keith the tools of the trade. Keith had only clippers, not the full complement of attachments and trimmers, which cost about two hundred dollars, money he didn't have. During the long days of banter with the shop's customers, Keith noticed how the owner seemed strong, a man of his word, full of a firm self-respect that made people look up to him, qualities Keith coveted. The barber told Keith that he was a member of the Tabernacle of Christ congregation, an evangelical Christian church in Newark, and Keith was welcome to come. A few weeks later, Keith gave it a try.

As the weeks passed, Keith regularly made the trip downtown to the church, in the notorious Hotel Rinaldi—after a double murder there, a warrant sweep had resulted in twenty-eight arrests. If Keith didn't have bus fare, he sometimes walked almost three miles from the apartment he was sharing with his brother. He went on Sundays during the day, at night, and on weekdays. He went so often, he was given keys to the front door.

On Halloween night 2004, a Sunday, the barber preached to a gathering of about ten, including Keith. At one point, the barber declared that in Christ there is abundant life, and the words resonated for Keith, who was desperate for salvation, not in the afterlife but in this one. He sat back, thunderstruck. He could not hear anything else. He had searched so long for the ladder to a normal, happy life, but the rungs fell away each time he'd get his footing. He was tired of searching and struggling and trying to soothe himself with drugs. He had given them up after his arrest, and he wondered whether Christ and a faith life could be his way forward. He walked up to the altar without his usual swagger and talked to God.

"If you could take this away from me, this feeling of dying— constantly just hurting and constantly not understanding and constantly just lost—if you take this lost feeling from me, I'll live for you. If you can do it, I give you my life, Lord."

Keith's conversion—that's what he calls it—lifted his spirits. He resolved to leave behind the street life and the false starts and focused on repairing his relationships, beginning with Mawson, who had wearied of his missteps. She encouraged his sobriety and his faith and welcomed him into her home when he needed a place to stay.

Keith's faith moved his heart in unexpected ways, as Jim discovered one afternoon during a conversation at Je's, under the wooden ceiling fans, stained-glass lights, and plastic hanging baskets. As Keith tucked into a plate of whiting with side orders of macaroni and cheese and collard greens, he mentioned to Jim that he'd like to find and talk to his birth mother one day.

"Okay, what would you do?" Jim asked.

"Talk to her, sit down, tell her I love her."

"That's amazing that you would even say this, that you could meet someone who left you when you were five and be able to express that."

"I don't have any ill will towards her," Keith said. "You want to forgive, to release people, and then you can move freely. Because I don't have no ill will in my heart, so I don't worry about it." For Jim, those words were deeply moving, yet impossible to understand. He realized that he could learn from Keith just as much as Keith had learned from him, and this education continues to this day. They live very different lives, but each sees the other as a friend and a teacher.

"I think me and Jim are like the same person," Keith said, "just in two different bodies, with two different lives, but with the same kind of heart and mind."

Two men whose fathers died tragically. Spiritualists yearning for God's grace in their lives. Boys who had pined to put their families back together. Encouraging each other, believing in each other. Making their imperfect road less grueling by walking it together.

DR. KENNETH GINSBURG ON FOSTERING
RESILIENCE THROUGH MENTORING

Dr. Kenneth Ginsburg is the medical director at Covenant House Pennsylvania and the author of Building Resilience in Children and Teens *and* Letting Go with Love and Confidence. *He describes what parents, as well as mentors, can do to bolster resilience in their children, regardless of their life circumstances: help them feel connected, competent, and confident; teach them coping skills and self-control; nurture their character; and help them contribute to society. To succeed in life, he says, young people need someone who believes in them unconditionally and holds high expectations for them. Often, that's a mentor.*

Don't forget what Covenant House is doing—in many cases, it's reparenting kids. Many of our young people never got the intense attachment they needed from their parents, and they became independent before they ever got the chance to become dependent. They've gained more maturity than many of their peers, and they have a resilience that most people will never attain. But these kids are hungry for close relationships, with people who are doing the right thing, who have no agenda other than for them to succeed.

You may not be able to repair young people to the point that they can be who they could've been if they had been raised in an appropriate, loving way and offered all of the resources every child deserves. If you dwell on that, then you'll never get engaged, and the kids need our involvement. What you're changing is a kid's life trajectory. Some will achieve great heights and have a real potential to serve others, precisely because of the life lessons they have gained through hardship.

You can make kids begin to believe in themselves again, by listening deeply for their strengths and reflecting their lives back to them through a different lens than they've used for eighteen or twenty years. They might share stories filled with risks and undesired behaviors, but I'm going to point out their resiliencies, their strengths—all the reasons essentially why I love them.

When they see their own strengths, it can combat the demoralization that has paralyzed them from taking action. Maybe they'll trust someone for the first time, and maybe in five years they'll let someone else reach out to them again, and they wouldn't have if you had not been involved.

The idea is, you believe in them and help them believe they are worthy of someone's caring. You may be working with a twenty-one-year-old, but behind him is a four-year-old hurting boy, a ten-year-old who's wondering why he got put in foster care, and a fourteen-year-old who did what he had to do to survive in a world you can't imagine. When you show someone he or she is worthy of love, that can be profoundly healing.

We cheat ourselves when we measure only simple statistical successes, such as living independently or finishing school. Our real goal is to fight the demoralization that gets kids stuck in a negative cycle. I believe in love. I believe love heals, and I don't believe you can accurately measure love and respect.

Lately, Jim has been coaching Keith on how to write a business plan for a mechanical repair company Keith is starting. When all of Keith's tools were stolen last winter in front of his apartment in Irvington, Jim chipped in seven hundred dollars to help replace them, provided that Keith paid two thirds of it back in sweat equity and paid one third of it forward by helping someone else in an emergency situation. The arrangement showed Keith that Jim had vital faith in his new business, and it fortified his resolution to press forward.

Seeing Keith today, it is difficult to imagine the defeated and strung-out adolescent he used to be, hustling his way through the streets. He wears his Afro close-cropped, in a geometric shape-up: neat triangles shaved along his temples. He favors crisply clean white shirts and wears a cross on a gold necklace. He is hoping to get a loan to expand his business and to buy a van, and he plans eventually to employ people who are coming out of prison. He wanted a new van, but Jim pointed out that it would become very messy very quickly, with the tools stored inside, so Keith is looking for a used one now.

"I wish everybody had a Jim," Keith says. "I just wish everybody that was in my situation had somebody who said, 'You can do this, and I'm going to believe with you.'"

The Power of a Presence

Be a mentor.

How do you count the kids who don't end up homeless because a relative, a friend, or the parent of a friend hires them or takes them in? It's nearly impossible. Yet kids, even those who have been through hell, can start to soar when they have just one steadfast person who believes in them and has high expectations for them. They do better when they have their own family plus a handful of other people who do that and best when they have a community to support them, but in many cases, it takes only one committed adult.

So, be a mentor.

Sometimes, well-placed advice can save a homeless kid from taking a very bad turn. There's a long list of things that many homeless kids don't know, because they haven't been taught.

Some don't know how long to get to know someone before moving in with them or becoming pregnant by them. Or they don't know how to manage a debit card or how generous they should be to their family and peers. Most of the kids at Covenant House have missed out on the bane of the adolescent's existence—the steady, loving, sometimes mundane, sometimes fraught checking-in that happens between parents and young adults: Whatcha doing today? Did you remember to sort your darks from your lights in the wash? Did you pay your phone bill? Did you call the dentist? When is that application due again?

The evidence continues to build that mentoring works. A randomized study of Big Brothers Big Sisters, the largest donor- and volunteer-supported mentoring network in the United States, found that at-risk young people in the program, compared to similar children facing adversity, skipped half as many school days and were about half as likely to use illegal drugs. The Little Brothers and Little Sisters also had slightly higher grade point averages, got along better with their families and peers, trusted their parents more, and reported being less likely to lie to them. A study in Canada found that 84 percent of Little Brothers and Sisters graduate from high school at a rate 20 percent higher than the general population.

Another study found that mentors helped kids to like school more and feel more competent there. Their grades and sense of self-worth also improved. A separate study showed that mentoring can have long-lasting effects on healthy living habits: adolescents who had been paired with an adult for guidance were significantly less likely to have used drugs in the previous month, to have had sex with multiple partners in the previous six months, to carry a weapon, or to smoke more than five cigarettes a day. Kids who struggled the most in school benefited the most from mentoring—lower-achieving students improved more than their higher-achieving peers did.

Mentoring programs have been shown to be effective with subpopulations of young people at risk of homelessness. Mentored kids who were at risk of juvenile delinquency or mental illness showed fewer behavioral problems than did those who had not been mentored. A study of mentoring programs for kids about to leave foster care found that mentors helped them feel less angry and helped them understand and be more open with their emotions. A 1995 study of impoverished teen mothers showed that mentors broadened the teens' social networks, giving them more opportunities for jobs, training, and education.

Research has documented ways to create strong relationships with young people who need guidance. First, mentors should expect slow progress—trust builds gradually. And make sure you can stick with the commitment you make—two studies of school-based mentoring programs found that young people whose mentors showed up inconsistently or for just a short period of time actually showed more behavior problems, less confidence about school, and lower self-esteem than they had before.

Yet adults who honored their commitments for a year or longer, for an hour a week or more, saw their young partners make improvements in academics, relationships, and behavior. The enthusiasm they feel for these successful matches is contagious, and the mentor movement is growing. More than three million young people were paired with mentors across the United States in 2008, a sixfold increase from a decade earlier.

The results can be significant. A mentor can help a kid find a job or give timely advice on a social predicament. An engineer can help a student pass the math section of his high school equivalency exam. A family with a van can help someone who just moved into her first apartment with grocery shopping or moving furniture. Some mentors even go on to adopt their mentees.

Covenant House has paired many young people with trained volunteer mentors to provide encouragement and moral support as they try to build a future. Keith and Jim's story is one such pairing, which has developed for more than a decade. Keith has a strong belief in such relationships and an appreciation for the patience it takes to build them.

"Being a real good mentor, you can save a life. Which will save other lives," he said, "which affects a generation. But you probably won't see it. You may be dead when it happens. Ain't nobody going to say it's going to happen next week."

6

Searching for Safety
Meagan's Story

Have you ever been hated because of who you are? Have you ever been rejected by the people you love most? If so, could you fight that hate with love and generosity, even if that put your own future at risk? Meagan learned the importance of honoring family obligations better than her family did. We ached as we watched her struggle, but her ability to love and forgive inspired us deeply.

No one knows for sure how Meagan's story will turn out. She has been in and out of Covenant House in Hollywood several times, a common rhythm when rebuilding a young life—a few steps forward, a steady job, a few steps back, after unsteady relationships take their toll.

One of Covenant House's central tenets is choice—once young people choose their direction, the staff supports them in their journey, even if it does not follow the most direct path. It's their future, and the staff helps them embrace it fully, as their cheerleaders, as their mentors, as people who care.

One way to know Meagan is through a tour of her bulletin board in her bedroom at the Covenant House in Hollywood. It tells the story of a young person clinging to her individuality, despite the heartbreak that exiled her to the streets. A huge

Oakland Raiders towel serves as her curtain. Sunlight filters down from a skylight in the high, angled ceiling, and the sounds of the nearby 101 freeway wash over the room. The carpet is an industrial gray, and the bulletin board hangs next to Meagan's pillow.

"That's my world," she said of the items on display, and it's a world of contrasts. She decorates with photos, Mexican flags, a little blackboard with pictures of the most Anglo Disney Princesses. There's a prominent picture of her mother, who stood by silently as she was kicked to the streets, and whom she nonetheless continues to help. She points out a bookmark of San Judas Tadeo, the patron saint of lost causes, whom she prays to when she's trying to go to work or save money or if she's feeling depressed and hopeless. She believes he helps her when she's low on cash.

There's a folded paper globe in the colors of the Mexican flag, because she loves her heritage and wants to give back to her community. In fact, a month after entering Rights of Passage, Meagan put together a Cinco de Mayo festival for other kids at the shelter. Her counselors watched her evolve from being a boss to being a leader, as she organized committees and dealt with people who had offered to help but didn't. She planned a Mexican dinner, posted descriptions of famous Mexicans around the kitchen and on the walls, and joined the staff in some traditional *folklorico* dancing. It felt like her birthday, she said.

Near the globe, Meagan has pinned a picture of her handsome late grandfather, wearing a plaid flannel shirt. She was only six when he died, and she flailed without the anchor of his steady, loving presence. Meagan's grandmother, the matriarch of the family, then started her slow descent into bitterness, and Meagan began to emulate her older brother, a troublemaker. Beside that snapshot is a picture of the artist Frida Kahlo, right next to a black velvet picture of Tinker Bell that Meagan colored with magic markers.

There's also a blue bandanna, the color worn by the kids hanging out in her neighborhood in Orange County, south of Los Angeles.

Although she says she was never involved directly in a gang, she is no stranger to the slang, the abbreviations, and the traditions. Neighborhood life meant shopping at the indoor flea market, occasionally fighting and shoplifting, getting tattoos, and going to car washes. "It keeps me at peace," she said in her tumbling, high-pitched voice, which doesn't quite match her tattooed, husky frame. She has shaved her eyebrows and penciled them back in, following the ultra-feminine, mucho-makeup *chola* style favored by some urban Latinas. She enjoys the split between who she is inside and the hard persona others see. She may appear intimidating, but she sees herself mostly as soft and sweet.

Underneath many of the pictures and the postcards, there's a bejeweled construction of kelly green netting—fairy wings, right above her bumper sticker for the Raiders. She loves the wings for being girly and pretty, almost as much as she loves the Raiders.

"You can still be beautiful and sassy," she explained, and it's a motto, though at times she doubts that she's beautiful.

One souvenir from her bulletin board reveals a clue to Meagan's heart, and it cost her the roof over her head—a crumbling red rose in a cellophane sleeve, from a girlfriend. When Meagan's grandmother found out that Meagan was gay, she kicked her out and threw all of her clothes in the trash, because the grandmother didn't want any "dirty lesbians" in the house.

Although about 4 percent of the general population is believed to be lesbian, gay, bisexual, transgender, or questioning (LGBTQ), numerous studies and surveys during the last decade have shown that sexual minority youth become homeless at a disproportionately high rate, with shelters in some cities reporting that they account for up to 40 percent of their residents.

Each year, an estimated 240,000 to 400,000 LGBTQ minors become homeless. Compared to straight homeless youth, they are more likely to be robbed or assaulted and three times as likely to be sexually assaulted or raped. Many feel exiled and deeply isolated. Their survival often depends on a homeless shelter.

Caring for such young people is a responsibility that shelter staff must take seriously, said Brian Bob, who has led Covenant House's outreach efforts to homeless teens in Hollywood, San Francisco, and Oakland and who currently works in New York City. "Parents have kicked these kids out and judged these kids," he said. "The issue is that you're homeless, not that you're gay or transgender. We're going to serve these kids with absolute respect and unconditional love, like it says in our mission statement." It's a sentiment echoed far and wide, from pop superstar Lady Gaga's recent "Born This Way" campaign to "Always Our Children," the 1997 pastoral message the United States Conference of Catholic Bishops sent to parents of gay children. In it they wrote, "God loves every person as a unique individual. Sexual identity helps to define the unique persons we are, and one component of our sexual identity is sexual orientation. Thus, our total personhood is more encompassing than sexual orientation. Human beings see the appearance, but the Lord looks into the heart."

Too often, sexual minority kids hear hate instead. Classmates, teammates, neighbors, even family members bombard them with messages of rejection, and far too many kids internalize those words. According to *Clinical Child Psychiatry and Psychology*, more than a third of lesbian, gay, or bisexual youth have attempted suicide, and they are up to four times as likely to do so as their straight peers.

Another way to get to know Meagan: ask her whom she calls "Mom." There's her mother, Maria, who left her four children several times for long periods. There's Louisa, her maternal grandmother, a strict disciplinarian who, despite serious health problems and several hospitalizations, raised Meagan and her three siblings when their mother left. Louisa, too, eventually turned her back on Meagan, kicking her out of the house three times before Meagan was twenty. There's also Rachel Cramer, who opened her Orange County home to Meagan after Louisa kicked her out of the house and who ultimately brought her to Covenant House California in Hollywood. Meagan feels she collected a couple more mothers there, too.

Meagan knows maternal love only in strobe flashes and snapshots, not as a sustained and unconditional force. Mothers go away, leave, push out; she has seen it often. Growing up, she didn't feel close to Maria, who would end a phone call not with "I love you" but with "Well, I gotta go." They didn't talk much. Yet Meagan misses her now, especially on lonesome days at the shelter.

Home still has a huge pull on her: the food, the smells, the way her family talked about the importance of family. She grew up in her grandmother's three-bedroom house with her uncle, a brother, and two sisters. Sometimes her mother, Maria, who battles depression, lived with the family; other times she didn't.

Louisa was the matriarch, virtually from the start. When Meagan was four or five, her mother got married and had two daughters by her husband, even though he used to beat her. It was an on-again, off-again relationship. Maria moved around, living with her in-laws in Mexico for a while, settling briefly in Las Vegas, and spending time in jail.

Meagan met her father, Juan, only three times—once when she was about ten, when a judge ordered him to visit her; once when she was thirteen, during court proceedings related to a paternity test; and next at sixteen, when she told him to get lost, once and for all.

At ten, she answered the door of her grandmother's house and somehow knew that the short, dark-skinned man with short hair, wearing khaki pants and a buttoned-up shirt, must be her father. In the big living room, she sat on the opposite side of the sofa from him. She didn't know him and was scared. After talking to him for a minute, something clicked for her. "I don't want you, I don't need you, I don't want anything to do with you, in any part of my life," she told him, and he left.

Maria's intermittent mothering, Louisa's poor health, and Juan's absence let Meagan fly under the radar. She came to see an upside to neglect, especially when carrying around a dangerous secret that could upend her life entirely: she was attracted to girls. She'd felt it since she was five or six and kept it locked away until the burden was too heavy. It was hard to have a secret she couldn't share with anyone at all.

Meagan remembers telling her mother she was gay, after talking to a therapist at middle school. She was only thirteen years old. On their way to a dentist appointment, Maria asked why she'd been speaking with the therapist. Meagan nervously blurted out, "I'm gay."

It was such a relief.

Meagan didn't understand why her vision suddenly blurred, why her eyes were watering. The sting of Maria's slap took a moment to register.

"You see tears before you feel them," Meagan said. "You don't even realize you're crying."

In the past, many gay and lesbian young people waited to come out to their parents until their twenties, when they no longer relied on family for shelter and sustenance, but that is changing. "There's no biological reason why a youth would come out at twenty-five," said Dr. Caitlin Ryan, the director of the Family Acceptance Project in San Francisco, California. Young people are, on average, eleven years old when they experience their first romantic attractions and fourteen when they realize they may be gay, she said, and the average age to come out is now sixteen, a vulnerable time. If that conversation doesn't go well, the young person can end up without a place to sleep. Sometimes that happens immediately; other times, the breakdown of a family is more of a slow-motion train wreck.

Soon after she slapped her daughter, Maria went to jail for two years for a crime Meagan can't remember. Meagan watched over her sisters, Alana and Stephanie, making sandwiches for them, brushing their teeth, and walking them to school. Maria came back unexpectedly, at four thirty one morning, hollering with tone-deaf enthusiasm for the kids to get up and come with her to the International House of Pancakes. But no one wanted to wake up that early on a school day. Meagan, then about fifteen, fumed at her mother's audacity after the many times Maria had followed other paths beyond the important one, being a mother to her four kids. The girls rolled over in their beds, too tired to indulge her whim.

Meagan's youngest sister, Stephanie, probably suffered the most from Maria's absences, often crying herself to sleep in Meagan's arms. Meagan and her three siblings come from three different fathers, and Stephanie's father was her grandmother's least favorite. Because Stephanie resembled him, her family treated her poorly and questioned Meagan for sticking up for Stephanie. Her grandmother kept telling Meagan that she had just one brother and sister, that Stephanie didn't count. This only made the two girls closer.

When Meagan turned seventeen, Louisa, short-tempered due to her declining health, bristled at Meagan's mouthiness and kicked her out of the house for the first time. As much as Meagan wanted to assert her emerging independence, her eviction was sudden and jarring. She couch-surfed, living with friends for a couple weeks, until Maria interceded for her with Louisa. In many respects nothing was the same again. Whenever Louisa disapproved of Meagan's behavior, she exiled her granddaughter for weeks at a time.

There were points when Meagan's despair over having no food and no shelter smothered her. Twice, she made half-hearted suicide attempts that she speaks about casually: "I tried drinking. That didn't work. Then I tried pills. That didn't work. Then I was like whatever, that didn't work. I give up. If God wants me to die, that'll happen. And if He doesn't want me to die, I'll still be here."

Her reaction is, unfortunately, not surprising. More than 60 percent of homeless lesbian, gay and bisexual young people try to kill themselves at least once, twice the percentage of straight homeless youth.

On a hot summer day in 2009, when Meagan was twenty and living back at home, her younger sister, Alana, told their grandmother that Meagan had posted something about a girlfriend on MySpace. If Louisa had suspected that Meagan was gay, she'd never let on, and now Louisa was simmering mad. Everyone had gone to bed, with Meagan sleeping next to Maria in Maria's room, hoping to get a good night's sleep before a job interview the next day. But Louisa woke Meagan at five in the morning, griping about some dishes that had not been put away. The argument moved to the living room, which was lined with pictures of family members, hanging on the walls and standing on the tables, ringside for the fight to top all others.

"How could you like girls?" Louisa yelled. "You're going to die. You're not going to amount to nothing in life! Leave my house and don't come back."

Meagan changed from pajamas into jeans and left at five thirty that morning with her phone, her phone charger, and some clothes jammed into a purse. Her mother slept through the fight.

As Meagan walked out of Louisa's home, past the courtyard of flowering bushes she once had found so calming, she felt devastated. *Oh, my God. Again?* she remembers thinking. *What do I do?*

She wandered around and ended up at her mother's workplace later that day, but Maria refused to intercede for her, because Maria was living with Louisa rent-free and did not want to jeopardize the arrangement. Meagan asked for fifty dollars for her cell phone bill. Her mother said no.

Meagan next met up with Stephanie, who had also been kicked out of the house recently. As they lived on the street together,

Meagan marveled at how her sister, whom she had mothered, turned the tables, showing Meagan such maternal tenderness, sneaking her into the homes of friends overnight, staying strong when guys pulled over and propositioned them, being a rock—a fifteen-year-old rock. Together, they rode buses to the end of the line and slept in a park by their grandmother's house. Meagan remembers the swings and how the monkey bars were shaped like a fort. Sometimes Stephanie stayed with her boyfriend; sometimes Meagan stayed there, too. It beat sleeping outside.

"You're out where there's bugs and it's dirty and there's drug dealers and ho's and pimps," Meagan said. "You're like, what if they want me to be a ho? What if I get caught up with drugs? What if I'm in the middle of somebody gangbanging and there's a shooting, or there's somebody randomly crazy that's going to kill you or there's an accident like a hit and run?"

Stephanie helped pull her through those long weeks on the street, but Stephanie wasn't looking for safety. She got in with the wrong crowd and landed in juvenile detention. Meagan started spending time with a friend, Thandi Cramer, and her mother, Rachel.

Thandi and Meagan had attended high school nearby, but they were not particularly close at first. After Meagan became homeless this last time, the friendship deepened. They became confidantes, and Meagan now refers to her as "my play-sister," the term she uses for a close friend. She laughs about that, because they don't look much like siblings—Meagan is short and curvy, with long black hair, while Thandi is tall and blond.

When Meagan was visiting Thandi's house one day, Rachel asked about her living situation, while they were watching television. Meagan didn't want Rachel to pity her but told her she had nowhere to go. Rachel, a cheerful woman who wears her curly red hair up in a high ponytail, told Meagan she was welcome to stay. After that, every time Rachel turned around, it seemed as if Meagan was doing dishes or helping out in other small ways.

For three months, they all lived in the small, two-bedroom apartment with the Cramers' two dogs, Meagan either sharing Thandi's room or sleeping in the living room. At the time, Meagan's sister Alana had a boyfriend who was homeless and staying at Covenant House in Hollywood. He said it was a good place, so Meagan and Thandi looked it up online. Meagan found the website, and Thandi read it, because Meagan doesn't like to read—a loss of oxygen to her brain shortly after birth left her with a learning disability. Thandi deemed it a place to make a new start, and Meagan decided to give it a try. She wanted to make Rachel, "the best mom I could ever have," proud of her. Ready to take charge of her life, Meagan did not want to impose on her friends any longer.

The two girls slept for barely half an hour the night before Rachel and Thandi drove Meagan up to Los Angeles, thirty miles away. She had visited the city only twice before, for baseball games. She tried to relax and put her trust in God.

"I think He said, 'Okay, you've done okay, I'm going to send some people to your life,'" she said.

Arriving at Covenant House

Thandi, Rachel, and Meagan all cried that afternoon in 2009 when they dropped Meagan and her two bags at Covenant House, within view of the Hollywood sign. The adobe building stands four blocks from Hollywood Boulevard, known for its drug addicts, johns, and pimps. Rachel worried that the entrance wasn't secured at night (it is), and Meagan was afraid she would never see the Cramers again (she did).

In conversations during the following days, Meagan unburdened, telling Covenant House counselors she felt sad and lonely most of the time and had felt that way for most of her life. Sometimes, she said, she didn't sleep for days. She was upset by a recent breakup with a girlfriend and nervous about how she'd do at her first home-less shelter, where she knew no one. She didn't want to fail—she wanted to stay strong. She was going to get her life on track.

She mustered the courage to call her grandmother and mother several times, but they told her never to call again.

Bobbi Rodriguez, an outreach worker at the reception center, is the first Covenant House person Meagan called "Mom."

"She had a lot of guards up," said Ms. Bobbi. Meagan told the staff she was gay but did not go into much detail about her family. "She portrayed herself as a quiet gay person. We found her people she could actually talk about it with."

Sexual minority kids who come to the shelter often need a wel-coming message more than the first good night's sleep. Dr. Kenneth Ginsburg, the medical director of Covenant House Pennsylvania, has seen quick and positive changes in some youth just from the new chance to feel accepted instead of shunned.

"So many of these kids are in trouble because of how much pain they've been in, because of the shame and isolation," he said. "Shame and isolation can be broken with love and respect. For that reason, the good we can do with an LGBTQ kid is enormous and relatively simple."

Meagan soon began to feel at home at the Hollywood shelter. She put her resume together and found a job working part time at a Mexican restaurant. She also began to find her place in the social life of the shelter and avoided some of the common con-sequences—an early curfew, extra chores—young people receive when they ignore their goals or the rules.

Even after Meagan earned a spot in Covenant House's Rights of Passage apartments in the back courtyard of the main shelter, behind the gardens with sculptures and fountains, she still checked in with Ms. Bobbi every few days. They have similar shaved and penciled eyebrows and bright blond highlights in their thick black hair, and Ms. Bobbi helps Meagan tone down her makeup.

deBorah Smith, fifty-three, whom Meagan called "Grandma," also helped her early on. When Meagan's mother cut off contact with her, it was Ms. deBorah, a counselor at the crisis shelter, who comforted her.

"She told me the people you live with and who raised you isn't necessarily your family," Meagan said. "She made it a lot better." When your original family rejects you, you can build a new one, as Meagan discovered.

Ms. deBorah enjoyed watching how Meagan flourished in massage therapy school, wearing a uniform, gaining a skill that could prove quite profitable. School was expensive, and Meagan was forced to use her savings and take out loans to enroll, but it was in pursuit of a livelihood, and she loved being good at something. Although Meagan had had difficulty in traditional school subjects, particularly math, she now had a vision of a career in which she could use her new skill to help others. Many of her clients told her she was truly gifted.

Yet home kept pulling her back, the home where she wasn't welcome anymore. Even though her family didn't want to talk to her when she called, if they ran low on cash, they were all too willing to contact her on her cell, manipulating her with guilt and the occasional "I love you." Few of them knew she was in a shelter, because shelters were against the family's unwritten rules. You couldn't keep your pride in a shelter, they felt.

Over time, her family seemed to need her more than ever. Maybe, she thought, they would accept her if she helped them, even if that came at the expense of her education. Maybe, eventually, she could go back home and fix what was broken.

It's another example of a child's birth ties being stronger than any blows and insults the parents dish out—that heartstrong desire to return home, to make things right, to solve whatever problems the child, rightly or wrongly, feels responsible for. Too many homeless kids such as Meagan have been cast aside by the people closest to them, but they show a loyalty and a generosity that could make them—like the other stones the builder rejected—the cornerstones of a wiser, more compassionate future.

Meagan wanted to see her family in Orange County, to give them cash, but a taxi would have cost a hundred dollars. She figured out a way to meet them in the middle via public transportation, to give them money she had saved. This didn't surprise Ms. deBorah. She'd seen Meagan take on other people's problems before managing her own.

"You break it up, baby, it is just too much for you to handle," she told Meagan. "That's the part that makes you become sad or depressed or overwhelmed, with too much on your plate. You have to take little bites, instead of big spoonfuls."

In the end, Meagan couldn't swing the combination of school and work, and her family kept calling with unpaid bills. She left school with fourteen thousand dollars in student loans but no certification to practice. School would have to wait.

There's a third way to know Meagan: take a tour of her tattoos.

First and foremost, her grandfather's name is on her left wrist. Growing up without a father, Meagan was extremely close to her maternal grandfather, with whom she lived. She remembers how he loved coffee and cigarettes and bananas and black beans and white rice, just as she does. She liked watching her grandparents take care of each other, with him cooking savory dishes and her grandmother making sweets. Her grandfather would come home from work as an engineer and hug and kiss her grandmother, who shooed him away playfully.

"I guess when he died, a part of me died, too," Meagan said. She was six at the time, and she remembers starting to rebel soon afterward, watching the more violent cartoons her brother liked, dressing the way he dressed, making him a replacement father figure, a role he could not fill.

"God wanted him," she said of her grandfather. "I can't be one of those people that are like 'I hate God because He took that person.'"

Her family told her he had died of cancer, but one day, a dozen years after his death, she discovered his death certificate. It said he had died of AIDS, which he had contracted in prison. Right then, Meagan gained insight into her grandmother's discomfort with homosexuality. If her grandfather were still living, Meagan says, maybe her grandmother would never have kicked her out of the house for being a lesbian.

"What if God were somehow to send him back to me? Would I be in Los Angeles? No, back home in Orange County. I'd be in school, working, I would have a car already and be financially okay, and I'd be mentally okay. But no, God wants me to go through all these obstacles and trials. He still has plans for me, to change somebody's life, to help somebody, to have my family."

On her grandfather's birthday, after she turned eighteen, Meagan commissioned a tattoo of her grandfather's nickname on the inside of her wrist.

"I wanted his real name, but I have small wrists," she said.

She went home to her grandmother right after that, wearing a long-sleeved sweater even though the day was hot. She asked her grandmother to cook up his favorite foods. As the kitchen heated up, Meagan left her sweater on, keeping her secret as long as she could.

"You're up to something. Take your sweater off," the older woman said. She put on her glasses and touched the tattoo in disbelief. Later, after her grandmother kicked her out of the house, Meagan had her grandmother's nickname tattooed on her other wrist. Louisa saw the tattoo and called her granddaughter crazy. But Meagan wasn't crazy; she wanted to cinch her grandmother to her, to prevent Louisa from ever pushing her entirely away.

"I would have nightmares when I was little and run to her room," Meagan said. "She'd stay up late at night, ironing everybody's clothes for Monday morning. I was nervous about school, and I had a nightmare and ran to her. She just held me in her arms. I was crying, and she was nurturing me, taking care of me, pampering me. That's where I get it from, the nurturing side of me." And outranking any other more recent mother figures, "Maria" graces her left instep. "If you really stop and think about it, lots of people don't have moms, don't even know them," she said.

In a way, by inscribing the names of her family on her skin, Meagan is trying to keep her people close to her, to create on her own canvas a permanent family portrait that her relatives and her circumstances can't take away from her.

Meagan recently took the bus to visit Louisa, who was recovering from surgery. Maria was seriously ill and living with Stephanie not too far away. Thoughts of mortality and something she had watched on television were weighing on Louisa's mind.

Seated in her bedroom, about to eat brunch, Louisa started talking about *Laura*, a daytime television show from Mexico she had watched.

The show featured a transgender man and his mother, who had hit him and could not accept him. He had been abused by other people as well, and later, the mother broken down in remorse. That struck a chord with Louisa, who had tears in her eyes as she spoke.

"After that, she felt bad," Meagan said. "She didn't want anything bad to happen to me. When she kicked me out, she was afraid I'd get AIDS and die, which is why she did what she did." With Stephanie and Maria out of Louisa's home, Meagan said, Louisa felt that Alana and Meagan were the only two girls left and she didn't want them to live apart. Louisa told Meagan it would be nice if she moved back.

"She was talking about how much she loved me," Meagan said. "She was like, 'Oh, I'm dying, I'm leaving soon. I don't want you to hate me. I don't want to hate you. Let's let bygones be bygones.'"

Louisa didn't quite apologize, but she had extended an olive branch. As for herself, Meagan felt surprised, happy, and sad all at once, sad that her big fight with Louisa had happened at all. Yet she didn't completely trust this change of heart.

MEAGAN ON HER MOMS AND HER FUTURE

Meagan says her Covenant House counselors have stood behind her as she struggled and have made her feel part of a family. Perhaps collecting so many people to call Mom helps Meagan fill the vacuum, as no single woman has ever mothered her in a reliable and enduring way. Yet now, at Covenant House, several are trying. Meagan is clear about the counselors' importance in her life, as she launches into a riffing imitation of their motherly concerns.

"What're you doing, where are you going, I don't like that outfit, take it off, why do you get a piercing, why's your eyebrow like that, did you eat, are you hungry?" I know these people. They would give their food for me and whatever they had for me, if they had to. I know they're good people—they only want the best for me. And if I were ever to fall into trouble, I know I could count on them. They're additional moms to me.

I guess I'm having hope that it's a better day. Because after all the bad stuff, you're always having that happiness at the end. At the end you're going to find that one person or that one item that's going to make you happy. If it's not music, it's books. If it's not books, it's that one person; if it's not that person, it's your family. If it's not your family, it's your friends or your coworkers, your play sisters or your mom, it really doesn't matter. Your niece and your nephews could be screaming at you, playing around, and you're like, "Wow, I'm really happy, I have a life ahead of me."

Meagan sits in her room at Covenant House and ponders her next move. She is tired of living in flux, but she worries that Louisa's invitation might be motivated by the $450 Meagan just sent from her paycheck. What if Louisa sends her back into the streets again? Meagan wants to be loved for who she is. She longs for reconciliation, had even been willing to buy her way into it, but she cannot stomach the thought of being homeless again.

"No more," she said. "I don't want to start my life all over again. It gets a lot harder."

The longer she stays at Covenant House, the more secure she feels there, the more she knows herself. The shelter, she thinks, has helped her break free of misperceptions, that old divide between what people—even family members—see and who she really is.

"Covenant House can mold you to the person that you should be, not to these ideas people have, that you are weird and a *chola*, and you can't accomplish something. In finding myself—me, who I am—I worked a lot. My entire life I hated school, but at massage school, I said, 'My God, I really like this. I can really do this.' I'd like to go back to school. It's me."

Where does Meagan really belong? The shelter is more welcoming, but her people and her roots remain at her grandmother's. "Home to me is like, not necessarily a home," she sighed. Would Orange County be easier? Louisa hadn't offered her complete acceptance, but it was a start. Meagan could sleep in her own bed. Even though her friends at Covenant House call her Sunny, for her outgoing ways, the pressure of homelessness is bringing her down. On a scale of one to ten for stress, she gives herself a twenty, especially on days when her late-night bus ride home from work takes two and a half hours.

She glances down to her right wrist and her grandmother's nickname, then looks around her room. Where, after all, is home?

Helping LGBTQ Youth

Lesbian, gay, bisexual, transgender, and questioning (LGBTQ) kids are overrepresented in the ranks of homeless young people, and they may often find adult shelters and the streets to be dangerous at worst and unwelcoming at best. It's often better for a young person to stay in his or her own home, whenever it is safe and healthy, than to start fresh with strangers, especially when social services resources are limited.

Yet how do you make a home more welcoming? How do you convince parents to accept their LGBTQ son or daughter? In its pastoral message to parents of gay children, the United States Conference of Catholic Bishops notes, "A shocking number of homosexual youth end up on the streets because of rejection by their families. This, and other external pressures, can place young people at a greater risk for self-destructive behaviors like substance abuse and suicide." The bishops offer this counsel: "Your child may need you and the family now more than ever. He or she is still the same person. This child, who has always been God's gift to you, may now be the cause of another gift: your family becoming more honest, respectful, and supportive. Yes, your love can be tested by this reality, but it can also grow stronger through your struggle to respond lovingly."

The research of Dr. Caitlin Ryan, the director of the Family Acceptance Project in San Francisco, offers many valuable insights about how parents can help their children through the process of coming out. Looking at 245 young adults, she studied the reactions that parents had to news about their children's sexual orientation. She found that young people whose parents had shown strongly rejecting behaviors were more than 8 times as likely to commit suicide, almost 6 times as likely to have been depressed, and 3.4 times as likely to engage in risky sexual behavior or use illicit drugs as those whose parents had been accepting. Compared to young people with parents who were very rejecting of their gay identity, those whose parents were only slightly rejecting were half as likely to attempt suicide, use illegal drugs, or take other serious risks with their health.

Dr. Ryan, who is not related to Kevin Ryan, saw that parents often expressed rejecting behaviors out of love for their children and concern for their safety. In many cases, they wanted to protect their children from the violent prejudices of society, so when they asked them to stay away from gay friends, act more masculine or feminine, or keep their LGBTQ identity a secret, they felt that they were acting in the child's best interest. They didn't know their reactions made their children feel rejected and unwelcome. Yet the parents truly loved their children.

Dr. Ryan understood that parents who felt very uncomfortable about their child's sexual identity still did not want their actions to endanger their child's health. (We saw this in action when Louisa wanted to make peace with Meagan after a television show about a transgender man who had been abused.)

Dr. Ryan spreads the word on specific ways to help. The Family Acceptance Project lists more than fifty accepting behaviors, such as talking to your children about their sexual identity, showing affection to them when they tell you who they are, advocating for them if they are mistreated because of their identity, connecting them with an older role model to show them they can have a happy future, or inviting the young person's friends and partners into your home. Taking even a few such steps could be good for your child's health.

Dr. Ryan has seen parents mourn when their children contracted AIDS, committed suicide, or were beaten up after leaving home following a family battle. She feels hopeful, though, because her research has shown that such rifts can be avoided.

Although LGBTQ kids need safe and welcoming transitional living programs, homeless shelters, and foster care placements, those cannot come close to providing the stability and love potentially found in most family homes. Dr. Ryan's research is some of the most constructive work toward strengthening the relationships of families in crisis, because it shows that both parents and children can benefit from shoring up a young person's family at a stressful time.

7

Separate Paths Uniting
Paulie Revisited

Not long after helping with the dinner for the kids of Covenant House Alaska, Paulie Robbins headed out from the restaurant where he worked, joined by his coworker Raphael, to pick up fish from a local market. Raphael's girlfriend, Courtney, a quick-witted firecracker, was working the register, and she and Paulie, a shameless flirt, talked for a while. Raphael seemed a little jealous and walked outside, which made Paulie and Courtney laugh. As they said their good-byes, neither of them knew that the long-lost son Courtney's sister had been searching for over the years was—heading out the door with several crates of groceries. Paulie had been flirting with his aunt.

Courtney's sister—nicknamed Frankie by their father, who wanted a son—grew up in Alaska with her father, because she and her mother didn't get along. At thirteen, Frankie took up with a much older boyfriend, who disappeared two days after she told him she was pregnant. Her father sent her to Washington State to live with her mother, though she tried to hitchhike back to Alaska. Barely a teenager, she gave birth to Paulie down on the Washington coast, and when Paulie was two months old, she lived with him on the streets of Seattle. If there had been a shelter for teenagers with new babies, she said, everything may have turned out quite differently for them, but child welfare workers sent them to foster care. Her father eventually took them back to Alaska. She raised Paulie for two and a half years, carrying him everywhere—he walked late because she forever hoisted him from place to place. He made a funny noise, pushing out his lips and breathing in and out to be silly, and it tickled her.

Frankie's father died of cancer when she was sixteen, and she was suddenly a homeless teen mother in the middle of Alaska. She asked Paulie's paternal grandparents to take him while she got back on her feet, but they gave him to the child welfare office within two weeks, without telling her. Soon afterward, the state persuaded her to let Paulie be adopted by Hank and Tiffany Robbins, a married couple who would take better care of him, she was told. She agreed, believing she would still be able to visit him, believing she had no other options. She wrote her son a farewell letter, pleading for his forgiveness.

At first, she remembers seeing him once or twice a year, usually including Christmas. She watched him from the street if she went by the Robbinses' trailer or saw him playing outside. When she found a babysitting job in the neighborhood and made contact with Paulie, Frankie said that the Robbinses called the police. She thought she could either give up trying to see her son or go to jail. Ever since, the state seemed to consider Paulie's a closed adoption and refused to help Frankie find him, even after he turned eighteen. She eventually left Alaska and her son behind.

Frankie had been searching for him during the last couple of years and had even traveled up to Alaska to see her sister Courtney and look for him. But the Robbinses no longer lived in the trailer home, and no one there knew Tiffany's whereabouts or her son's. During one search, Frankie grieved over a death certificate for a Paulie Robins about the right age. Later, she realized she had been spelling his name wrong for years (two Bs!). She typed the correct spelling of his name into Facebook, and Paulie's face smiled back from her screen. It had to be him; his mischievous eyes hadn't dulled in more than two hard decades.

When Paulie received a phone call in 2010 from a woman claiming to be his birth mother, he was ecstatic. Was this, at last, her? He was no longer in communication with Hank, whom he had forgiven years earlier, but he called Tiffany—now clean and sober—in Ontario. Her response was muted, because the news broke her heart. Paulie and Frankie exchanged a series of phone calls, each less tentative than the one before it. Some lasted for hours.

Contact with Frankie invigorated Paulie, kindling in him a hopefulness about his future. He relayed the full story to Deirdre Cronin, the executive director of Covenant House Alaska, with whom Paulie had kept in close touch since helping with the holiday dinner. He was brimming with anticipation.

As Paulie readied to meet his mother, Deirdre encouraged him to come by for a cup of coffee. He was flush with pent-up longing and curiosity. She talked through the possibilities with him, trying to prepare him for any outcome.

Privately, the idea of a reunion gave Deirdre pause as she mulled the irony and the tragedy of this mother and son: once upon a time, homeless and adrift as teenagers in Anchorage, both cut loose by their mothers, virtually fatherless, stripped of their childhoods, shaken into a new reality at the age of thirteen. Separated by time and distance but connected by blood, Paulie and his birth mother lived parallel lives. What they could become for each other if reunited—a buoy, an anchor, or something in between—was unpredictable.

After twenty-two years, Frankie and Paulie met at the Delta baggage claim in O'Hare International Airport in Chicago. Frankie, still suffering from a long-ago broken promise that she could stay involved in her son's life, could finally hold the young man she had last seen as a preschooler. Paulie, who had grown up believing Frankie had left him in a shed as a baby, bent down a bit to embrace this mythical tattooed lady. They folded into a bear hug a minute long. Frankie cried, later regretting her choice to wear mascara, which ran. She has permanent mascara tattooed on anyway and much more noticeable art on her body as well, including one piece celebrating her sobriety that took twenty-two hours to create.

They talked about finding food—Paulie was hungry and trying to put on weight. He was very graceful and kind in his interactions, telling Frankie, when she disparaged herself, that she was beautiful. He told her not to apologize for the older vehicles she drove. It's all good, he said.

Frankie, who is forty and has a Midwestern drawl, had just finished a monthlong haul as the driver of an eighteen-wheeler. As she drove a Ford sedan she'd borrowed from her sister, she talked about what they could do during their visit—go to the zoo or to Six Flags.

"I hope we get one good storm, so we could do the storm together and sit out," she said, though she promised not to put him in harm's way. Frankie had a friend who could take them fishing in the Mississippi, and she loves camping, but Paulie said he's a big city boy. Every time he goes into the forest, it seems he gets hurt, as if the earth is out to get him, he said. He figures he spent enough time outside. He likes showers and well-fixed food.

They headed to a small rural town where Frankie is living temporarily with her mother. On the way, Paulie talked about his plans for the near future, but he didn't mention moving to Illinois, something they had discussed before meeting. She prompted him about it, and he said that was the plan, for December, not November, as originally discussed.

Every so often, they looked at each other and smiled. Frankie had this way of closing her eyes slowly, like a cat in sunshine, basking in the moment.

"I think I have your lips and your chin," Paulie said. "I do. I've never been able to say that before."

She said he has his dad's eyes and nose.

"I hate my nose," Paulie said. "But it got less big the more weight I gained, it seems."

Frankie told Paulie his birth father's name is Edmond, and that he was nineteen, six years older than she was, when Frankie got pregnant. "It was my first time," she said.

"The first time you ever had sex you got pregnant? That sucks," Paulie said.

"It's all right, you came," she said. "It was a blessing."

They talked about how they had been born in the same hospital and were delivered by the same doctor, who offered to draw a clown face on Frankie's belly while she was laboring, which had infuriated her. They also discovered that they had another institution in common, the McLaughlin Youth Center, Anchorage's juvenile jail.

After the Ford's air conditioner lost its battle with the July heat, they pulled into a Burger King off Interstate 57, and Paulie asked her about the story he had long heard: had she abandoned him in a shed when he was a baby? Frankie told Paulie how the state social workers had told her that because she was a homeless teenager, she could no longer mother the son she had nurtured for two years. She did not know the origin of the story about the six-month-old in the shed, but she knew it was untrue.

Paulie tried to reassure her that things turn out for the best: "It's all good, we're here now." He doesn't talk much about the emotional pain he went through. He's trying to live lightly, he says.

After allowing Paulie to be adopted, Frankie saw other teen moms raising their kids, and she felt duped. Reeling from the loss of her son, she spent years struggling with substance abuse and heart disease. She nearly died twice, once from a drug overdose and once from a bout of salmonella. She has three daughters, two of whom she lost to foster care until she cleaned herself up. Her daughters were angry that her addiction eclipsed such a large part of their childhood, much of which they spent tending to Frankie when the drugs made her sick. She has been sober twelve of the last fifteen years and has two and a half years of sobriety now. Her fifteen-year marriage had just ended, and after her three girls decided to live primarily with her ex-husband, Paulie's arrival was a well-timed gift.

THE DEATH OF DECAL

—Kevin Ryan

When we work with homeless kids, we face the stark knowledge of their high risk for suicide, given their susceptibility to depression, anxiety, and broken family relationships. Rarely, a young person commits suicide at a Covenant House shelter, and when that happens, the aftershocks strike the kids and the staff with brutal force. The grief washes over us in waves, but we cannot run into a corner and mourn. A houseful of kids needs us, more than ever.

When I first started working with Covenant House, I'd spend time with Father Steven Siniari, an outreach worker for our Atlantic City shelter, looking for kids who needed a home and, above all, people who care. An Eastern Orthodox priest, he explores boarded-up buildings and what the kids call "The Underwood Motel," the shadows beneath the boardwalk. I trust Father Steve; he senses things others don't. He knows when kids are hurting, even when they say they are not. He also has an uncanny radar for where kids huddle and lurk if they don't have shelter. I have turned to him for wisdom and guidance through our low moments. When we lost one of our boys, Decal, to suicide in 2009, Father Steve, his voice choppy with anguish, found the wick among us and lit the flame we followed out of the darkness.

The death remains a mystery for Father Steve, who, with graying rusty hair, has a strong whiff of Bruce Springsteen to him, that is, if the Boss peppered his rock anthems with Greek theological terms. Father Steve told me about the word *eschaton*, which means "the end of the present world."

"I never worked for an agency or for a child," he said. "I always work for the life of the world to come." He figures the people who worked with Decal lost an argument with the young man, their words of encouragement outweighed by his despair. "Maybe in the *eschaton*, we'll learn that at the last moment there was some redemption, or there will be other kids who didn't go that route because of him."

Father Steve, who slept in Philadelphia's streetcars as a teenager, then told us about Vincent, a kid he had visited in a tool shed in a nearby suburb during the winter. The shed had no running water, and a wooden box served as a refrigerator. There were two swaybacked sofas and posters around the tools on the wall, near a handwritten moan: "I don't deserve to live like this."

Vincent had never set foot in a Covenant House shelter, but one of our central missions is reaching out to homeless kids wherever they are. After Father Steve helped Vincent search for a nice apartment a short distance from the shed, Vincent told him how he had almost killed himself. He'd wrapped his leather belt around his neck. But he'd had a friend named Bill who'd committed suicide. Vincent saw him, right at the last minute. Out of the light came Bill, saying, "No."

No. No.

Just maybe, Decal could serve that purpose for some-one else. We are all connected, Father Steve explained.

The hair tingled on the back of my neck as he stressed the importance of stories, how the story of the first boy Covenant House hadn't had room for, back in the early 1970s, haunted the agency's founder so much that our open-door policy was born. Because of that kid, we do our best so that no other kid should be turned away.

"Maybe the parable of Decal will bless someone not even born yet," he said.

"Amen, brother," I replied, wondering how I could borrow some of his hopefulness and share it with others.

Months later, I found myself looking for a donated outreach van to help us search for street kids in Asbury Park, New Jersey, Covenant House's newest site, a gem on a part of the Jersey shore battered by increasing gang violence and poverty. Next to me was Alex Siniari, one of our street outreach workers and, not coincidentally, Father Steve's son. I asked Alex what his dad had said to encourage him to help us reach disconnected kids.

"It's not what he said," Alex told me. "It's what he did."

His words reminded me that hope is a powerful contagion, more likely to be unleashed in all the right places by the things we do, not the words we say.

Paulie wants his adoptive mother, Tiffany, and Frankie to speak, to have a good relationship, but Frankie is trying to get over her anger that Tiffany did not protect Paulie from Hank. She also feels distressed to hear that Tiffany had told Paulie that he had been bounced from foster home to foster home before his adoption.

In the background as they ate their burgers, the stereo played that oldie by the Foundations, "Baby, Now That I Found You."

They finished up and headed back to the Ford. Its air conditioning had surrendered for good.

Frankie returned her sister's car and piled Paulie into her Dodge pickup with 160,000 miles on it, no muffler, and no air conditioning. She was in a rush to meet up with her daughters, who had been texting Paulie all day. With the windows down all the way to St. Louis—it was still ninety-four degrees at ten o'clock—it was too loud to hear the radio. Frankie was used to so many hours at the wheel, but Paulie felt exhausted after his red-eye flight from Alaska. He fell asleep with his head on her shoulder. She smiled her peaceful, feline smile.

Their reunion is still under construction, with frequent phone conversations and Facebook postings. Frankie had Paulie tattoo his name on her right wrist during his visit, and when he moves down to Illinois to be near her and his sisters, he plans to have her tattoo "mother" in Italian on his left wrist. But love and trust take time to grow. They are familiar strangers now.

"I don't expect finding my mom is going to fix me or anything. I don't need to be fixed—I don't feel broken," Paulie said. Yet he knows there is a type of love that endures in the world, and someday, whether as a son or perhaps as a husband and a father, he wants to share in it. "I've seen glimpses of what family means. What it's supposed to mean. I'd like to see more than a glimpse. I'd like to live it."

From watching so many young people struggle into adulthood, Deirdre, from Covenant House, knows that some wounds are so deep, the marks of the stitches don't ever fully disappear. She understands that Paulie and Frankie share many of the same scars, none of which can be covered with ink.

"Who knows what the future holds for them?" Deirdre said. "Maybe they will help each other heal. Maybe they'll reopen each other's wounds. I don't know, none of us do. They're in God's hands. That's where they have been, even through all of this, and that's where they'll stay."

8

What You Can Do
Steps to Help Homeless Young People Thrive

Homeless young people need to know that someone believes in them, and a variety of efforts, large and small, can help them significantly as they struggle to find a brighter future. Here are some ideas for what you can do to help.

Mentoring

Perhaps you can become a mentor and, through regular shared meals, phone calls, e-mails, or even texts, provide encouragement, company, and advice to make a difference in the life of an ambitious young person.

If you would like to work intensively with homeless young people, Covenant House offers a yearlong volunteer opportunity, the Faith Community, a corps of committed advocates, many of them recent college graduates or empty nesters, who want to make a difference in the world for kids at risk. Started thirty-five years ago, the Faith Community still attracts scores of volunteers to work full time as trained youth advisers or case managers with our kids in Anchorage, Atlantic City, Fort Lauderdale, and New York. Community members commit to live simply in service and prayer, and they receive room, board, medical and dental insurance, vacation, college loan deferment, and a severance stipend. Most important, they get to see miracles, big and small, unfold in the kids' lives. For more information, check out CovenantHouse .org/FaithCommunity.

You can work schoolwide or district-wide to help homeless kids graduate from high school. The Youth On Their Own model can work in any number of schools and takes only one full-time person. Are you a retired teacher or manager? It could be a second career! Or you can tutor a homeless teenager, work with groups that support young fathers, or teach young parents skills for raising their children.

Anti-Trafficking Efforts

What can individual citizens do to fight the scourge of trafficking? We can start by teaching our children about respectful relationships, making sure that they know that sex is about love and respect, not something that can be bought and sold. Boys need to know that buying sex won't make them men.

There is much advocacy work to be done to bring about stricter punishments for those who traffic children and for the adults who buy their bodies. In Canada, advocates are needed to push for a more reasonable definition of trafficking, to facilitate prosecutions. In the United States, more states need to pass safe harbor laws, so that young trafficking victims will be met with help, instead of handcuffs. In addition, recovering survivors need more comprehensive services. Learn more at AbolishChildTrafficking.org.

Parents and schools must also educate kids about the warning signs and the ruses traffickers use to recruit their victims, such as pretending to become a boyfriend, often waiting until the victim feels as if she is in love and isolated from friends and family before forcing her into sexual exploitation. Young people who do not have a trusted adult they can turn to for advice are more likely to fall for such deception.

You can distribute flyers (PolarisProject.org/PublicizeHotline) about trafficking hotlines to bars and hotels, where trafficking victims can see them. Before the 2012 Super Bowl in Indianapolis, groups of nuns contacted the managers of 220 hotels and motels within a fifty-mile radius of the city, and educated employees to recognize and report possible incidents of trafficking. Such work can be done in any city or town with hotels or motels. You can also join the effort to urge hotels and travel organizations to adopt the Code (TheCode.org), a pledge to be vigilant about reporting suspected cases of child sexual exploitation. According to Benjamin Perrin, whose book, *Invisible Chains,* describes trafficking in Canada, corporations should be encouraged to prohibit employees from purchasing sex acts while traveling on company business or using corporate assets, infractions that could be punishable by dismissal.

Finally, the next time we read or hear about a sexually exploited person, we would do well to shut out the voices that cause us to judge and instead try to imagine the depths of despair, violence, and coercion he or she has been forced to endure.

Supporting LGBTQ Youth

You can fight hatred in the form of homophobia and transphobia, to help gay, lesbian, bisexual, transgender, or questioning young people find an easier route to adulthood, beyond bullying, depression, and prejudice. You can volunteer at a program such as the Family Acceptance Project, Covenant House, or LifeWorks at the Los Angeles Gay and Lesbian Center, where LGBTQ kids gather for support and fellowship, and learn from adults, both gay and straight, that a fulfilling future is possible. You can start a similar program if there is none in your area. For high school students, whether you are gay or straight, you can become involved in your high school's Gay Straight Alliance or Anti-Bullying Alliance or start one, if needed.

If you have a child who is a sexual minority, you can join or talk to a parent support group such as Fortunate Families, which provides peer counseling to parents whose children have recently come out of the closet. Maybe you will work with Parents, Families, and Friends of Lesbians and Gays (PFLAG) or faith-based groups that support young LGBTQ people.

Advocacy Work

If you like writing letters to the editor or to your elected representatives, homeless young people need your energy and eloquence. Has your state submitted a plan to the U.S. Department of Health and Human Services to gain access to federal funds to allow young people to stay in foster care beyond age eighteen or to help provide aid for guardians who take young relatives from the foster care system into their homes? Find out at FosteringConnections.org, and if not, ask your governor and local representatives why. Readers who are moved to take political action can write letters asking state officials to improve child welfare systems and provide more comprehensive transitional services and housing for foster children as they turn eighteen and beyond.

You can join in fighting for more substance abuse and mental health treatment for parents and young people. You can speak out to reduce the stigma around mental illness or decide to become a court-appointed special advocate (CASA), to represent abused or neglected children in court. For more information, check out CasaForChildren.org.

In the Community

Do you dream about running a marathon or a half marathon or competing in a triathlon? Through our Home Team (Covenant House.org/HomeTeam) of athletes who train together and raise money together, you can help Covenant House kids while landing a spot in races that can be very hard to join.

You can host a candlelight vigil for homeless kids. A vigil brings together members of your community at a local house of worship, a school, a park, or a public gathering place to raise awareness about, and funds for, homeless young people. To do so, check out Candlelight.CovenantHouse.org. School service clubs and religious groups have also held Solidarity Sleep Outs (SoliditySleepout .org), where predominantly school-age volunteers raise pledges and sleep outside to protest youth homelessness. In 2011, Covenant House started the "Solidarity Sleep Out–CEO Edition," in which fifty leaders in the business, sports, and entertainment worlds slept outside for our kids, raising awareness of their needs and dollars to help support them. In 2012, the Solidarity Sleep Out–CEO Edition will expand significantly, as hundreds of leaders plan to gather on November 17, 2012, in more than a dozen cities to withstand the elements and, for one night, sleep outside in unity with the hundreds of thousands of young people who struggle to survive on the streets. More such events are planned for future years, so keep an eye on CEOSleep.org for details.

How about hiring a homeless young person, such as a Covenant House resident or graduate? A steady job is one of the surest steps a young person can take on the path out of homelessness. Or maybe you'll take on the joyful work of helping someone practice for job interviews, move furniture into his freshly painted new apartment, or equip her first kitchen. The world is full of people who have a van to lend, who can spend a free afternoon to be a sounding board, or who excel at planning menus and cooking nutritious, affordable meals. Chances are, you'll receive more from the experience than you give.

Covenant House kids and residents of other shelters for homeless young people have basked in the energy of generous volunteers. You can lead a yoga class, give manicures, bring popcorn and a movie to play at the shelter, renovate or paint a room, or run an Easter Egg hunt or a pumpkin-carving contest for Halloween (the kids are still kids, after all, and many missed out on childhood rituals, such as birthday cakes or holiday decorating). Make cookies with them, throw a barbecue, help with resumes or budgeting classes, or organize a picnic or a field trip. At the beginning of the month, bake cupcakes for the kids who have upcoming birthdays.

You can have family and friends donate "gently used" professional clothing—it is vital that the kids dress for success when going on job interviews, and the right outfit can go a long way to help boost confidence and make a great first impression. Hold a drive to collect dress, casual, and athletic shoes; socks; and toiletries for homeless kids in your community. Like your children, grandchildren, nephews, and nieces, Covenant House kids outgrow their shoes at an alarming rate.

If you live near New York City, you can volunteer with Covenant House's NINELINE, 1–800–999–9999, or its website, Nineline.org. Young people in trouble call or contact the site for referrals and for help with issues such as abuse, homelessness, bullying, relationships, suicide prevention, and human trafficking. Volunteers are trained to counsel young people and refer them to help, via a database of thirty thousand agencies around the United States.

The needs of homeless young people are countless, and no dream of contributing is too ambitious—every Covenant House welcomes volunteers eagerly, and the staff is ready to help. It can make all the difference to a young person who does not know what it feels like to be cheered for and valued, but who still has time to learn that his or her dreams are attainable and that someone cares.

What You Can Do from Your Computer

Post banners about the issues facing homeless kids on your favorite social networking sites (see CovenantHouse.org/action/grassroots for more information). Become a friend of Covenant House International on Facebook, Twitter, and MySpace, and help us spread the word about youth homelessness.

Become an advocate for homeless youth and stay informed about breaking developments. Check out CovenantHouse.org/action/ambassadors.

Join Covenant House's Abolish Child Trafficking efforts, via AbolishChildTrafficking.org, and receive updates on child trafficking legislation and action alerts on how you can fight the sexual exploitation of young people.

Join the conversation on Twitter by using the hashtag #whatishome, as we ask friends, celebrities, and homeless young people about what home means to them.

On the Home Front

There's one ultimate action you can take to help prevent the pain and trauma of homelessness—maybe you'll be inspired to take in or adopt a foster child. Thousands of children go to bed each night without a forever family. When they look ahead to their future, they see no place to go for holidays, no refuge from hard times, no arms to hold them. If welcoming a young person into your home sounds too hard, maybe you can convince your religious community to take on the mission of both fostering children and supporting foster families. FaithBridge Foster Care in Georgia has worked with nine churches committed to such work, and their model is growing.

Ideally, the stories in this book will remind you how closely children listen to the messages they hear at home, how much they yearn for a loving and supportive family. All of us can be better parents, and one way is to ensure that our children know, on a daily and nightly basis, that they are loved and valued beyond measure. Surround them with family members, teachers, mentors, and friends who feel the same way. Find new ways to remind them that they are loved—it is the greatest gift they can receive. There is no down side, and you just can't say "I love you" enough to a child.

Keep Us Posted

Finally, please let Covenant House know what actions you take as a result of reading this book. Post them on CovenantHouse.org/AlmostHome, where you may be able to find people in your area who are also volunteering their time and efforts for homeless youth. All of those efforts, banded together, can help improve the chances that homeless young people can grow into the bright futures they deserve.

To Learn More

All God's Children: The Bosket Family and the American Tradition of Violence, by Fox Butterfield.

Breaking Night: A Memoir of Forgiveness, Survival, and My Journey from Homeless to Harvard, by Liz Murray.

Girls Like Us: Fighting for a World Where Girls Are Not for Sale, an Activist Finds Her Calling and Heals Herself, by Rachel Lloyd.

Growing Up Fast, by Joanna Lipper.

Invisible Chains: Canada's Underground World of Human Trafficking, by Benjamin Perrin.

It Gets Better: Coming Out, Overcoming Bullying, and Creating a Life Worth Living, edited by Dan Savage and Terry Miller, based on the videos that can be seen at ItGetsBetter.org.

The Johns: Sex for Sale and the Men Who Buy It, by Victor Malarek.
The Lost Children of Wilder, by Nina Bernstein.
Rachel and Her Children: Homeless Families in America, by Jonathan Kozol.
Random Family, by Adrian Nicole LeBlanc.
Somebody's Daughter: The Hidden Story of America's Prostituted Children and the Battle to Save Them, by Julian Sher.
There Are No Children Here: The Story of Two Boys Growing Up in the Other America, by Alex Kotlowitz.
Very Young Girls, a film about GEMS (Girls Educational and Mentoring Services), shows up-close the work of the agency, which helps young women who have been sexually exploited gain independence. It can be a great jumping-off point for a movie-night party, followed by a discussion with friends about the issues.

In addition, please consider sharing this book with your book club, house of worship, or social organization, so that more people can come to learn about the journeys of Covenant House kids.

Epilogue

Since we finished reporting for the book, Paulie met his birth father, found out that he is mostly of Native American descent, and is pursuing a business degree at an online college. Muriel has been accepted to college to study juvenile justice, with the goal of becoming a lawyer working on behalf of young people. She has strengthened her relationship with her family and is doing volunteer work with homeless animals. Benjamin is now married to the love of his life (yes, he found her) and received a promotion to work in a new school, where he coaches football and track. Creionna has received a promotion and moved from her apartment complex, Keith is getting married, and Meagan is in massage school full-time. Please check back at CovenantHouse.org for further updates about their lives.

In a recent conversation, Benjamin's mother said that even though she isn't in touch with him, she admires his strong will and ability to do what he sets his mind to. She said she had asked his forgiveness for burning his hands, and that he had forgiven her. And she said if she were in touch with him, "I would tell him I love him. I would tell him I miss him. I heard that he got married and, you know, I would welcome her."

The young people have made great progress in a short time, thanks in part to the help of the unconditional love and respect they received from people who cared about them, both outside Covenant House and within. Their stories remind us that kids need someone to believe in them, someone to love them, even if it comes long past their early years.

Notes

Our primary sources for demographics of the young people who stay at Covenant Houses are "A National Picture of Youth Homelessness: Characteristics of Youth Served by Covenant House in the United States," available online at http://www .covenanthouse.org/about-homeless-charity/institute/resources/ youth-crisis-report, and the "National Youth Status Report," available online at http://www.covenanthouse.org/images/pdf/reports/ ysr_national.pdf, both released by the Covenant House Institute in 2010. The Menninger Foundation's "Project Connect and Assessment Project," 2000, by Peter Fonagy et al., available online at http://www.casa-alianza.org/pdf/MenningerExecSummary.pdf, provided helpful information about where former residents of Covenant House live and their socioeconomic successes and challenges shortly after leaving the shelter.

For a discussion of health problems among homeless young people, we relied on the federally funded "Facts on Trauma and Homeless Children," 2004, by Ellen L. Bassuk, M.D., et al. from the National Child Traumatic Stress Network, available online at http://www.nctsnet.org/products/facts-trauma-and-homeless-children-2004.

Information provided by the Coalition against Trafficking in Women helped inform our recommendations about ways to fight sex trafficking.

For an in-depth discussion of the issues facing the Texas child welfare system, we consulted "Forgotten Children," 2004, by Carole Keeton Strayhorn (then the Texas state comptroller), available online at http://www.scribd.com/doc/38352706/Carole-Keeton-Strayhorn-Texas-Comptroller-Forgotten-Children-2004, and the lawsuit filed by Children's Rights in 2011 against Texas's child welfare system, known as *M.D. v. Perry,* available online at http://www.childrensrights.org/wp-content/uploads/2011/03/2011-03-29_tx_complaint_final.pdf.

For our understanding of what happens to foster children, we were helped by the PolicyLab at the Children's Hospital of Philadelphia and its groundbreaking research on placement stability. Useful statistics on trends in the foster care population came from the Administration for Children and Families, available online at http://www.acf.hhs.gov/programs/cb/stats_research/afcars/tar/report18.htm.

Helpful information about young people aging out of foster care can be found in a 2011 study from the New School's Center for New York City Affairs: "In Transition: A Better Future for Youth Leaving Foster Care," by Abigail Kramer, Kendra Hurley, and Andrew White, available online at http://www.newschool.edu/milano/nycaffairs/publications_cww_19and20.aspx.

We are indebted to both Mark E. Courtney's work at Chapin Hall at the University of Chicago, on long-term Midwest evaluation of foster care alumni, available online at http://www.chapinhall.org/research/report/midwest-evaluation-adult-functioning-former-foster-youth, and to the Casey Family Programs and its foster care alumni studies, available online at http://www.casey.org/resources/initiatives/FosterCareAlumniStudies/. "Time for Reform: Aging Out and on Their Own," 2007, by the Jim Casey Youth

Opportunities Initiative, available online at http://www.jimcasey youth.org/time-reform-aging-out-and-their-own, was also insightful.

A 2007 report from the School of Social Work at the University of Victoria, "When Youth Age Out of Care—Where to from There?" by Deborah Rutman et al., available online at http://socialwork.uvic .ca/docs/research/WhenYouthAge2007.pdf, was very useful.

UNITY of Greater New Orleans, a nonprofit homeless advocacy organization, provided useful background for our reflections on homelessness in that city in its 2011 report, "Homelessness in Greater New Orleans: A Report on Progress Toward Ending Homelessness in the Years after the Nation's Largest Housing Disaster," available online at http://unitygno.org/wp-content/ uploads/2011/06/PIT-2011-Report.pdf.

For our research on the effectiveness of mentoring programs, we found very helpful the "One-to-One Mentoring Literature Review," March 2007, by Keoki Hansen of Big Brothers Big Sisters of America, available online at http://oregonmentors.org/ files/library/BBBS%201-to-1%20Mentoring%20Literature%20 Review%20_Mar%202007_.pdf.

We found valuable information about homeless young people who are lesbian, gay, bisexual, transgender, or questioning in "An Epidemic of Homelessness," 2006, by Colby Berger et al., online at http://www.thetaskforce.org/reports_and_research/ homeless_youth. Research by Dr. Caitlin Ryan provided incredibly useful information for families of LGBTQ young people. In particular, her article in the January 2009 issue of *Pediatrics*, the journal of the American Academy of Pediatrics, titled "Family Rejection as a Predictor of Negative Health Outcomes in White and Latino Lesbian, Gay and Bisexual Young Adults," was helpful, as was "Supportive Families, Healthy Children," a description of how families can help support their LGBTQ children, available from the Family Acceptance Project website, http://familyproject .sfsu.edu.

Index

NOTE: Page references in *italics* refer to photos.